STOP OVERTHINKING STARTING TODAY

Exercises and techniques to relieve stress, anxiety and eliminate negativity

Max Cureton

Copyright 2023 All rights reserved©.

The contents of this book may not be reproduced, duplicated or transmitted without the direct written permission of the author. Under no circumstances shall the publisher be held liable for any legal responsibility or liability for any repair, damage or monetary loss due to the information contained herein, either directly or indirectly.

Legal Notice:

No part of the contents of this book may be amended, distributed, sold, used, quoted or paraphrased without the author's consent.

Disclaimer Notice:

The information contained herein is for educational and entertainment purposes only. No warranties of any kind are expressed or implied. Readers acknowledge that the author is not engaged in rendering legal, financial, medical or professional advice.

INDEX

Foreword	7
Being grateful makes you happy	13
Here and now	19
How to be positive?	25
The energy that comes from meditation	31
Compare yourself only with yesterday's version of yourself	39
Complaints and criticisms	47
Awareness of unconsciousness	53
Pleasure for pleasure's sake	61
Choose wisely the battles to fight	69
High vibration	77
Balance	83
Positive discomfort	89
What happens if you aid another person?	95
Sometimes, less is much more	101
The method to achieve abundance	107

An objective reading of the situation	113
Law of attraction	119
Try to feel more and think less	125
Final reflection	129

FOREWORD

First of all, I would like to extend to you a warm welcome on this voyage that will, starting now, be solely under your control. Sincere congrats for having the guts to put time and effort into your own personal development and maintaining your own inner calm. Those that have the courage to venture outside of their safety zone and have the ambition to continue on their path are fairly rare, so kudos to them. You are courageous, and you have a lot to offer both to yourself and to the people you care about the most.

When we live facing an excessive number of distractions, we are more likely to engage in the pattern of overthinking. To put it another way, when we fail to live in the here and the now. So, let's get this straight: what does that imply? If we think more than we feel, then we are not living in the moment; if we live with sorrow about the past or worry about the future, then we are overwhelmed with feelings of grief, anxiety, guilt, wrath, and resentment... and we overthink.

What is essential for us to realize as quickly as possible is that the human brain does not distinguish between real-world experiences and those that are only imagined. The sensation you get when something actually takes place in your life is identical to the one you get when you anticipate it taking place. Therefore, you need to start taking into consideration that strength so that you may use it to your benefit. The great majority of our concerns are unfounded or do not materialize to the extent that we fear they would. Therefore, instead than fretting about it, you should get busy. Act rather than react to the situation.

When I say to avoid responding, of course, I mean reacting in a bad way, since that is what I mean when I say to avoid reacting.

It's possible that you'll conclude that certain chapters in this book have little to do with the overthinking problem that the book primarily addresses. But each of them, in their own unique way, makes a direct contribution to the calmness and serenity that you experience on the inside. They will also assist you in concentrating your attention on the here and now, gradually lessening the mental chatter that you experience, and providing you with the equilibrium and well-being that you require.

Let me assure you that none of the ideas that I will be discussing with you in these pages are completely foreign to me. Through my own personal experience, out of need, curiosity, and conscious choice, I have learned all of them, absorbed them, put them to the test, and ultimately incorporated them into my life because of the power they have and the wonderful outcomes they produce. In addition, I continue to put many of these strategies and secrets into practice on a regular basis in my day-to-day life since there is always something else I can get better at or learn to make me happy and more appreciative.

Believe me when I say that I would never be so dishonest as to provide you something without first determining whether or not it is effective; after all, what use would it be to you if I did that? as well as what use would it be to me? What good would it do for me to exhibit something to the world that I'm not even sure is true or if it has any practical application?

If someone were to teach me anything, I would have a moral obligation to pass on that information to the next person in order to ensure that the information does not become obsolete. If I tried it, and found that it was helpful to me, then it would be right for me to do so. In a similar way, there will be information that I have either unearthed on my own or that is the method of another person that I have versioned in order to adapt it to me, and as a result, I adapt myself to them.

At the very least to some degree, the majority of these strategies or experiences are connected to one another and may be seen to either complement or impact one another. When you have internalized and put some of these insights into practice, you will notice that your perspective has shifted, that you are able to notice details that you had previously missed, and that what was previously unclear or incomprehensible about the world or yourself now feels crystal clear and easy to comprehend or put into practice.

"The mind that opens itself up to a new notion can never go back to the size it was before".

Albert Einstein

Back in the day, I couldn't wrap my head around a few of the ideas that I can now explain with ease. I had not long begun my journey toward personal improvement, and there was a great deal of material for me to take in. And thankfully, I still have a lot to pick up along the way. But such is life, and it is such a brilliant teacher that if you don't learn a lesson, it will repeat it again and over and over and over until you do. If you don't learn it the first time, it will keep doing it until you do.

The beneficial feature of implementing any of these strategies or ideas into our day-to-day routine is that as soon as we assimilate them and begin applying them, we will see improvements in ourselves regarding a variety of factors. For instance, physical activity not only makes one healthier but also helps one's mind and spirit feel more uplifted. The practice of meditation not only helps to relax the mind, but it also lowers blood pressure, which in turn will enhance circulation, focus, positivity, and other aspects of your life. And in the same way, with each new chapter of this book, we have the opportunity to set off a very potent and beneficial ripple effect that will assist us in growing on all fronts.

Sincerity is the only thing that can forge a genuine connection between two hearts. This book connects my life to yours and serves as a bridge between us. One of the most effective and attractive ways for individuals of different cultures to communicate with one another. I will not be the one to cast doubt on the longevity of that bridge or raise concerns about its potential future.

Because of this, I owe it to my word, my beliefs, and my consistency to provide you with material that is shareable and that you can use to further your own personal development.

When I came to the realization that this information was useful to me, that it functioned well, and that it assisted me when I required it, I became convinced that I ought to disseminate it to a greater number of others. On the other hand, as we all know, hardly nobody will let themselves be assisted by another person until they specifically ask for it. It appears as though it would be impolite to accept assistance from another person. It would be almost the same as admitting that you couldn't figure it out on your own, as publicly confirming that you don't have the knowledge they want to give you, or as stating that you need help, and of course, in the world that we live in, admitting that you need assistance could be considered "weakness."

But, my good friends, the truth is that we are all more or less knowledgeable about a minimum of facts in life and totally uneducated about practically everything else. To put it another way, we are experts in practically nothing and students of everything. And why is it that we have such a hard time recognizing it? Because of one's pride, dignity, or concern about one's appearance? I'm not sure what the most popular explanation is, but it makes no sense to me why people do it. We all, and I repeat, we all, need or potentially require the appropriate aid at the right moment. Do we seriously believe that the richest people in the world, who are considered the most "successful" guys on the globe, got where they are entirely on their own and without the assistance of anybody else? No, sir, I don't believe that's the case.

"If you walk by yourself, you will cover more ground in a shorter amount of time; if you walk with others, you will cover a greater distance".

Proverb from China

As a result, I think that there are times when we need to relax our guard a little bit, at least when it comes to learning, allowing ourselves to be affected by others, putting our egos aside, and listening to what others have to say. We need to have the ability to listen without feeling the need to reply. In order for us to comprehend, we need to get better at listening. to put ourselves in the shoes of the person who is speaking and to try to comprehend what he has been through.

And in order to progress and learn new things, we need to have a healthy amount of skepticism, not just about what we already know but also about ourselves. This is the only way that development and progress of nearly any type can be achieved. Because of the absorption of new knowledge, which, when combined with your DNA and the rest of your experiences and facts, will result in the creation of new methods and a beneficial evolution of both your being and the world around you.

Have the courage to discover your optimal level of well-being. Your body will feel light and resistant, your energy will be fluid and overflowing, your attitude will be positive and joyous, and your life will feel different, full of happiness and abundance when you reach this ideal, maximum level.

Let us let ourselves go. Let's quit trying to be something we're not and just be what we are. Let's give in to our feelings and quit overanalyzing everything. At this precise moment, there are no problems to report. In this instant, there is complete and utter quiet, and nothing takes place. When we already allow the mind to engage, it fills the space with clutter. When this happens, it might be difficult to locate whatever is no longer in its proper location.

BEING GRATEFUL MAKES YOU HAPPY

Everyone has the ability to cultivate a sense of gratitude toward others. It does not involve a significant amount of effort or a significant amount of time investment, yet it has the potential to change our lives and our view of it in a completely revolutionary way.

When we express gratitude for all that we have, we train our minds to be more conscious of the blessings that are all around us. We are concentrating on the positive aspects. We are able to highlight the numerous great things that are happening in our lives right now.

That "what you focus your attention on is what you attract or extend in your life" is something that most of us have probably heard at some point in our lives. But I'm sure that each and every one of us has heard the saying that "misfortunes never come alone." Isn't it hilarious? They are essentially the same thing seen from two different perspectives. If I dwell on the negative, then more negative things will occur. On the other hand, if I choose to concentrate on the positive, only nice things will occur. And if you or anyone else in your vicinity truly is unable to recognize the positive things that are happening around you, you ought to take a deeper look. Alternately, try looking out of a different set of eyes.

It's possible that we are under the impression that nothing nice is taking place or that there is nothing great going on right now that we are able to notice. However, there is none. You have arrived. Simply the fact that you are still alive is remarkable in and of itself. The idea that you can breathe on your own is an intriguing topic of discussion. You are able to read these lines, you had breakfast this morning, you slept warm, someone greeted you in the morning, you came home from work, you have money to cover your needs, you had a delicious dinner last night, you can walk using both of your feet, etc. etc. etc. etc. etc. etc. etc. etc. etc. etc. etc. etc. etc. etc. etc. etc. etc. etc. etc. etc. etc. etc. etc. Do you still believe that there is nothing that could possibly be considered positive in your life?

There is no need for any of us to compare our lives to those of other people. In point of fact, it is unpleasant, as the proverb says, but let's do it for the sake of simplicity for a little while. How many people live in abject poverty across the globe? How many are suffering from hunger, cold, being in the thick of a conflict, and other conditions? And in spite of all of this, they have the widest and most beaming smiles that are humanly imaginable on their lovely faces? Wow... it's definitely something to sit quietly and reflect on. Who are we to judge between those who have "so little" and those who have "so much"? They laugh as they go around barefoot in the muck, while we wail in our "castle." The Western world, sometimes known as the first world, struggles with issues such as depression, boredom, and sloth. These issues are the result of excessive behavior. By the excess of joys that are shallow and transient, by the excess of stimulation that are meaningless and temporary, and by the excess of comfort. A reassuring yes. Both creativity and the growth of the human race are stifled by routine and comfort.

When we have more, it makes us want even more. And the more we want, the less value we place on what we have.

"Not he who has the most is richest, but he who needs the least".

St. Augustine

It is not a matter of having insufficient resources. Or perhaps it already is. It all comes down to how much value you place on what you have and who you are. It's not about getting everything you want; it's about wanting everything you already have.

When you are able to recognize the boundless wealth that is all around you, you will realize that everything is going according to plan. It is sufficient in every way. Everything that happens is a blessing, a fortune, a luck, a gift, and a treasure. Nothing bad ever happens. And you are the fortunate one who gets to take advantage of it. Put away the blindfold and quit thinking that other people have "more" than you do by comparing yourself to them. Look at the chapter titled "Pleasure for the sake of pleasure" to learn why not everything that sparkles is actually worth your time and effort. Not everyone who is considered wealthy lives a happy life. But by practicing gratitude, you can find happiness in life. It is not necessary to have a million dollars in order to be considered "wealthy." When you are sitting in the park and feeling the sun on your face, you can get a sense of the good fortune and enormous plenty that you have in your life. Or going for a walk with your pet on a Sunday while it's raining. Or going for a swim in the ocean or a pool and experiencing how your body floats somewhat defying the force of gravity.

Brother, it is good to see you! The fact that we have arrived already provides a lovely sensation, don't you think? Tell your thoughts to take a break and concentrate on the here and now; aren't there a myriad of things for which you should be grateful right this very moment? Then you should give thanks. to everything, including the universe, God, the Buddha, and Allah. to your own mother and father, as well as to your own daughter or son and any brothers or sisters you have. to your next-door neighbor, to the baker, and to the person you work with. Whether one is alone or with others. Say it, and experience the transformative power of appreciation. Notice how the universe immediately returns its energy to you when you feel grateful, and the hairs on your body stand on edge as a result. This occurs when you both express gratitude and make it known to others. And you do all of this not only because you want to bring more positive experiences into your life, but also so that you can recognize and appreciate the many positive aspects of your life right now, without having to wait for them to arrive.

Exercise: When we first get out of bed, let's get our bodies moving with a basic workout. Let's go find a place to sit down and relax once we've refreshed ourselves by drinking some water and using the restroom or brushing our teeth. Put your hands over your heart and close your eyes. Your right hand should be on top. Take a few calm, deep breaths, and focus on feeling your body as you do so. Now is the time to give thanks for everything that you desire. whatever it is that you consider to be a source of blessing or good fortune in your life. Give thanks for your life, for food, for your home or your job, for your family and friends, for your health; give thanks for having grown as a person or for wanting to grow; give thanks for being generous or determined; give thanks for being sincere or sensitive; or simply give thanks for the desire to give thanks.

The immediate sensation ought to be one of extreme positivity. The powerful message that we are grateful for all that is around us is being communicated throughout our entire organism, including the mind, the body, and the soul. Every cell in our body receives the knowledge that we are healthy, joyful, and surrounded by plenty. This information is transmitted to every cell in our body. It's a beautiful thing that's happened. In addition to this, the cycle has a self-sustaining positive feedback loop.

Perform this exercise every day for the next month and pay attention to how your behaviour, your attitude towards other people, and how you react to difficulties or situations that might normally have a negative impact on you change. I am confident that it will enable you to look at everything from a new perspective and strengthen both your optimistic and courageous mindset.

This practice will transform the lens through which we view life and will positively program your subconscious so that, over time, the thoughts that pass through our minds unconsciously and automatically become happier and happier, and they do nothing but reaffirm our happiness.

HERE AND NOW

"Stay present in the moment". "Carpe diem". "Make the most of the now." "Have fun with life". We've all been exposed to these marketing cliches, but are we able to actually put them into action?

We live in an age where we are inundated with information and stimuli, where there are hundreds, if not thousands, of ways to obtain fresh 'knowledge' immediately and from practically anywhere in the world. This is the age in which we find ourselves.

But how should we feel about that? They say that too much of something is bad for you, and I would agree that this is true in the majority of situations. Personally, I believe that having access to an excessive amount of information is detrimental for two reasons:

First, the information that is obtained is not given any value at all since there is an excessive amount of it and it is utilized in such a short amount of time that it is gone in the blink of an eye. While we are working to complete the processing of it, we have already begun to receive the following one.

Second, they completely disengage us from the here and now. They are a constant source of distraction, and although though advances in technology and information can bring us closer to loved ones who live far away, these advancements can also make us feel more disconnected from those who are in our immediate vicinity. By acting in this manner, we remove ourselves from the present moment, which is the only thing that can truly be said to "belong" to us.

Imagine for a second that a child is born into an affluent household. The family has a lot of money. On her birthday and at Christmas, she is showered with a mountainous amount of presents, of varying sizes, hues, and prices, each and every year. No expense is spared in this endeavor. Her parents want their daughter to have the best and to lack nothing, or perhaps they believe that this is a good way to educate their daughter, surrounded by what appears to be an abundance, even if it is simply material. Either way, they want their daughter to have the best and to lack nothing.

The majority of the time, the child will mature into an entitled brat who is unable to have any sense of appreciation for anything. Because he has been exposed to so many different stimuli and presents, he quickly becomes bored with them all. He has to constantly expand his experience in order to maintain the joy he gets from doing things like receiving presents or shopping for new shoes. Everything revolves on hormones and the impact those hormones have on the human brain. It doesn't take long for that rush of dopamine to wear off, and after a while, you start to feel a void in your life, which drives you to seek out more and more stimulation so you don't have to reflect on what's going on. It is undeniably an addiction, as well as a highly widespread problem in the modern world. In the following section, "Pleasure for the sake of pleasure," we will go into further detail on this topic.

Now, let us consider the scenario from the opposing point of view: a child who is born into a lowly family that is on the border of poverty, in which everyone contributes to the home tasks, and in which they consider themselves quite fortunate if they are able to put food on the table once or twice a day for the entirety of the month. The tiny child adores lending a hand to her mother and father. Because there is no television in the house, she passes her time by conversing with her mother, reading, and playing with her one and only doll, which is somewhat worn out and no longer has its string attached to it. Imagine the delight on her face if, by some stroke of good fortune, her parents are able to set aside some cash in preparation for her birthday and buy her a brand-new doll. She will cheer up by jumping for delight, doing circles around the living room, and hugging her parents while sobbing tears of joy and expressing her gratitude to them. This youngster is not accustomed to the kind of stimulation that is being presented to her, so she does not live unconsciously, consuming without any sense of self-control. Instead, her mind is focused on the here and now, and she lives in the moment without any distractions or meaningless pleasures. As a result, she places a high value on the things that are bestowed upon her, the experiences that she has, and the life she leads with her parents. This youngster has the potential to grow up to be a good person who is content with having very little or even less.

This is exactly what takes place in the here and now. We are subjected to such a vast array of stimuli and such an abundance of information that comes to us through our mobile phones, social networks, emails, calls, movies, series, work, news, and the press... that, for example, having dinner with our partners no longer feels meaningful or useful. This is because we live lives that are characterized by absentmindedness, distraction, an excess of meaningless stimuli, an imbalance of dopamine, and living on autopilot. And in point of fact, the things that we fail to see may very well be the things that are the most important.

If you are content with your life, it will not benefit the major advertising corporations in the least. They are successful if you buy and use their items and if those activities cause you to experience a momentary and ephemeral sense of "happiness" or, more accurately, pleasure. But if you've got a smile on your face, brother, a pair of torn clothes or an outdated mobile phone won't be able to take it away from you.

If you lay a strong foundation for your happiness, your life will be steady and meaningful, and you won't need temporary or phony motivation from outside sources because you'll have already established that foundation.

And you won't require the most recent mobile phone, the trendy T-shirt, the fragrance worn by the famous actor, or the automobile that is advertised on television. You will already be at peace and finished with everything. And, in the event that you ever make the decision to purchase any of those things, you will take pleasure in them and value them for what they are, namely, something fleeting and material that in no way contributes to your sense of identity nor has any bearing on the level of happiness that you experience.

Exercise:

Touch the nearest wall if you find yourself becoming distracted, upset, or especially when bad ideas come into your head. While you are doing so, make sure to take some slow, deep breaths. Now, direct your attention to what you are experiencing: is the wall hot or cold to the touch? How about a rough surface? When you put your hand on it, what does it feel like? firm? controlled? supportive?

And now, please tell me where that bad idea or fury that has engulfed you is now.

This is an effective method for enhancing our mental capacity so that it does not corrupt us. It is a method of showing it that there are certain things that it believes we don't like and that we don't intend to listen to it when it reminds us of them. This is a way of showing it that we don't like certain things that it thinks we do.

If this is not the case, do you believe that the great men and women who have achieved success become successful as a result of listening to their worries, insecurities, and negative thoughts? I don't.

"Although it is impossible to change the past and start over, it is never too late to make a new beginning in the present".

Carl Bard

Let us take a few moments to reflect on the following: now is the time when everything happens; now is the time when we can do something for our future; now is the time when we must do things that make us proud today and will make us even more proud in the future. Be the director, the performer, and the playwright of the movie that is your life; don't wait for other people to tell you what it will be about.

"There are just two days in a year in which you are unable to carry out any activity. The first is known as yesterday, and the second as tomorrow. As a result, the

present moment is the best time to love, to act, to develop, and most importantly, to live".

Dalai Lama

HOW TO BE POSITIVE?

They will tell you, "You need to have a positive attitude". But sometimes it might be pretty challenging. Especially considering the times we've been living in as of late. Because of this, it is more necessary than ever before for us to learn how to generate, to feel and transmit positivity, and to have it as our primary attitude towards life, because it may benefit us in more than one and in more than ten situations every day.

There are some things in life that do not, or at least rarely, go according to plan. The results are not always what was anticipated, and if they are beyond our ability to influence, the resulting repercussions are not always pleasant. At the very least, this is how we have become accustomed to perceiving things. How often have we heard, though, that "every cloud has a silver lining"? And from my perspective, there is a lot of truth to be found in that phrase, because many good things come after incidents that we judge as being "evil".

"There was a problem with my car". The fact that the mechanic needs to be paid and that we'll need to find an alternative mode of transportation while it's being fixed is, of course, disappointing. If we want to make it to work on time using public transportation, we'll have to get up a little earlier than usual. But if we keep our spirits up and strive to maintain a positive attitude, maybe after leaving the car at the garage, instead of rushing to the subway and forgetting about it, you decide to enjoy the moment and relax, and you invite yourself to breakfast at a coffee shop that you've never been to before; and then, all of a sudden, you run into an old classmate that you haven't talked to in years! You talk about the good old days, catch up, and then out of nowhere, an opportunity to collaborate on a professional endeavor presents itself to the two of you. Wow! Unbelievable, right? It's for the best that my automobile broke down.

Let's look at another picture: You've been working at the same place for the past five years, and although today is a new day on the calendar, servicing clients feels like second nature to you. Doing the same old operations, uttering almost the same old phrases, being bored or lacking motivation... But if you snap out of the loop you're in, pay a little attention to the present, and make an effort to be friendlier than normal, or ask the customer about his life or his day, everything will miraculously change for the better! Instantaneously, everything becomes significantly more interesting and pleasurable; you speak about anything and everything, discover things you have in common, share a few jokes, and laugh, even though you haven't even met each other yet! It's possible that this will also introduce you to new people with whom you can build your business relationships. And all of this is a direct result of making an effort to maintain a cheerful attitude and focusing on the here and now.

It is true that many thoughts emerge spontaneously from our mind and that we have no influence over these thoughts, at least not at the moment. However, what we can choose to do is decide whether or not to pay attention to these thoughts as they come up.

"If there's something you don't like, the only power it has is your attention. Take that away from it".

Carolina Herrera

Exercise:

Ignore any negative thoughts or feelings that surface when you are aware that they are making their way through the thin veil that separates your subconscious and your conscious mind. You should concentrate on anything else instead. Do some housework, sing, get some exercise, turn up the music, and dance. I find that humming is helpful. My mind keeps muttering unfavorable or discouraging things, and I find myself singing those thoughts. a tune that was made up, a tune that was known, it doesn't matter. "Nana nananaaa nana nana nana nana naaa..." and suddenly it disappears. The negative notion is no longer present. Because it is sick of you ignoring it, it has decided to leave. You have prevailed in this engagement, but the conflict will not end here. The key difference is that you are now equipped with the appropriate defense strategy to emerge unhurt from the situation. No opposition, complete acceptance, and focus on feeling more while thinking less.

I pay attention to what the mind has to say, but if it can't offer me anything beneficial, I quickly shift my focus to something else since I'm not interested in what it has to say. I give myself a kind smile, then either write out my to-do list for the day or begin to warm up for my workout. In the following chapter, "Present Contact," we are going to go deeper into this consciousness.

Observe every time you experience or rather believe something that is bad or that does not provide anything beneficial to you or to others. This is an additional strategy that may be used to re-educate our thinking. Analyze it. If you get this feeling, you should ask yourself the following questions and find the answers right here in your book:

Exercise:

Why do I have this impression?

Do I truly believe it, or is it merely a meaningless outburst that has nothing to do with what I think or what I would like to do?

Is this an example of productive or destructive thinking?

Is it beneficial for myself or for others if I articulate this idea out or if I take some kind of action in response to it?

And, maybe most importantly for me: if I am witnessing the appearance of a thought, who exactly is it that is thinking it?

My point of view is that we make a significant error when we conflate our minds with who we are as individuals. Our conscious awareness is under the control of our subconscious, and our subconscious in turn is under the control of the sum total of our life experiences and the knowledge we have learned. There are representations, ideas, laws, and facts that are ingrained in our subconscious, yet the majority of the time, we are not conscious of their being there. But they have a significant impact on how we behave, how we respond to things, how we evaluate things, and how we live our lives. I believe that there is more than sufficient motivation to want to continue researching more on the topic. Especially if we are aware that there is some unconscious, impulsive action or attitude that is not serving either us or people who are in our immediate environment, this can be very difficult to do. The moment to educate oneself couldn't be better. to be observant, analytical, accepting, and open to practice in order to progress.

"The wound is the spot where the light enters".

Rumi

Or, to put it another way, every event that we go through has the ability to provide us with the education that we require. But only if we keep our wits about us. When we be meek and pay attention, the universe unfolds before us and reveals all of its boundless opportunities. And always keep in mind that the grin is the one thing that all of the people on this earth can understand and communicate with one another through.

Do you believe that it is a waste of time and energy to concentrate on being optimistic?

THE ENERGY THAT COMES FROM MEDITATION

What are your thoughts on the opportunity, power, and strength you have to improve your well-being and health simply by shifting the way you think about things? It's a wonderful idea, isn't it?

We are able to alleviate some of the strain and anxiety that comes with living life by practicing meditation. We forget the concerns that follow us around, and when we are forced to confront them again, we do so with a fresh perspective. We provide the opportunity for ourselves to reestablish a connection with our inner nature, which is the source of our serenity and sense of well-being

"The Buddha was questioned regarding the benefits that he had obtained from meditation. Nothing, was the response he gave. On the other hand, I can assure you that I no longer suffer from feelings of rage, worry, melancholy, insecurity, or fear of becoming old or passing away".

Buddhist wisdom

Alterations that take place in our bodies as a result of meditating include: lowering of blood pressure, which results in an increased sense of calm; and activation of specific regions of the brain that are associated with love, empathy, and compassion.

- o It helps us become more coordinated and more focused, as well as improving our memory and our emotional steadiness.

- Alleviate the signs and symptoms of depression and anxiety.

There are currently a great number of scientific studies that back up the use of practices like these. Scientists are now able to clearly identify the regions of the brain that are affected while meditating thanks to the development of brain scan tests. And the outcomes are extremely satisfying and promising in every way. Therefore, there is already convincing evidence from the scientific community that meditating regularly grants us the ability to alter our thoughts. And to a much greater extent.

Other beneficial effects that can be attributed to regular meditation:

- Facilitates a more restful night's sleep for us.
- Relieves muscular strain.
- Reduces levels of the hormone cortisol, which is produced in response to stress and anxiety.
- Because it increases the amount of oxygen in the body, it lowers the risk of developing cancer.
- It facilitates disconnection and the relaxation of the psyche.
- Has a positive impact on our health in general.

I am of the firm belief that we ought to engage in regular meditation practice beginning at a young age. Because not just on an individual level, but also on a collective scale, there would be dramatic shifts in both the quality of our lives and the ways in which we interact with one another. There is no doubt that civilization would progress in a way that is beneficial to its relationship with nature and give more attention to the impact that it has on the surrounding environment. We would likely take better care of ourselves, we would also eat with more awareness, and we would adhere to an alkaline diet if we could do it without inflicting such severe suffering on the billions of animals used in agriculture and industrialized processes.

And this is only possible with a small amount of time each day set aside for you to sit quietly, focus on your own well-being, and let go of whatever tension you may be feeling. Doesn't appear to be all that difficult, does it?

The beginnings of a meditation practice

No one is ever born with knowledge. At some point, we are going to have to begin, just like everyone else, and begin learning. The process of learning is an invaluable asset since it assists us in maturing into better versions of ourselves and better prepares us for the experiences that lie ahead.

Have fun with this unique experience that has the potential to deliver you many benefits that will help enhance your health and well-being in a way that is completely natural.

Sitting with your back straight and listening to soothing music, preferably music without lyrics, is all that is required to accomplish this. Enjoy the moment of tranquility that you have created for yourself by slowly and deeply breathing in while also making an effort to feel more and think less. It's not about suppressing your thoughts and feelings of guilt for doing so, because those things come naturally. It is about being able to focus our attention on the music, on our body, and on our breathing when a thought comes into our heads and then not giving that thought any attention at all. Aromatherapy and the use of essential oils are two other ways that you might assist yourself in the beginning.

In the following paragraphs, I will demonstrate several distinct types of meditation for you to begin practicing:

The following are some different ways to meditate:

- Simply observing a photograph, a drawing, or the wall itself is an example of looking at an image. We will be able to achieve a state of relaxation and peace by breathing in a slow and deep manner.

- Mantras can be listened to or spoken; either way, keep this in mind: energy is vibration, and so is music. Listen to music that is relaxing or recite mantras, and you will acquire the pleasant and serene energy that you are looking for. This is one of the purposes of meditation, which is to raise our vibration.

- Concentration on the breath is the kind of meditation that is practiced the most frequently or is the most well-known, although most people find that they respond more favorably to a particular form of meditation. Feel the air entering you as you inhale, and then feel the air leaving you as you exhale. This is all you need to do. Focus your attention on the path it takes, the sensation it gives you, and the overall sense it gives you.

Perseverance is the single most critical factor in any endeavor, and seeing results is no exception to this rule. I promise you that over time, you will witness tremendous improvements in our way of being and acting, and that these improvements will be for the better.

These are some of the most fundamental approaches to the practice of meditation. But there are also other variants of them, as well as combinations of them; the important thing to remember is that in order to practice any of them, you will need to have a calm setting that is free of interruptions and engage in deep breathing.

Commence a regular practice of meditation:

- o Do some practice on your own: investigate, get a feel for it, and experiment with the various modes; you'll find that it's rather fascinating.
- o Read a book or watch a video tutorial: since we live in the information era, you have a multitude of options to gain the knowledge you seek; all you need to do is get started.
- o You should seek the advice of a buddy who is familiar with meditation; you must definitely know someone who meditates or someone who knows someone who meditates. There is no room for making excuses if you want to accomplish something.
- o Take a class: There are probably hundreds, if not thousands, of different meditation and mindfulness classes that are offered in different parts of your country. You can sign up for one of these classes today. Learn as much as you can about it and give it a shot. You have a lot to gain and very little to lose by doing this.

Pranayama Meditation

I would want to demonstrate one of the meditations that I have found to be the most helpful and enjoyable when I first began practicing. This is a form of Pranayama meditation, and it is a fairly straightforward practice.

Exercise:

Relax your shoulders and keep your back straight while you sit with your legs crossed. While breathing in gently via the other nose, one of your nostrils should be covered. Now open up that side and close off the side through which you were breathing in air. Slowly exhale from the side that is exposed, and then, without making any sudden movements, breathe back in via the side that you initially used to breathe in. Change sides. And this goes on.

Take some slow, deep breaths while appreciating the peace and quiet that is all around us.

This kind of breathing helps to balance the two hemispheres of our brain in a manner similar to that achieved by reciting the famous OM in a mantra. Because of this, we will have an easier time maintaining a healthy energy balance, and we will have no trouble entering a deep state of relaxation.

Practices of meditation in motion

You'll notice that you're calmer over time, that you sleep better, and that it's easier for you to avoid getting stressed out. Or perhaps you are no longer in such a rush to go to work, and as a result, you are able to take more pleasure in the drive or the music that is playing on the radio.

Exercise is a strategy that can be practiced at any moment of the day, and it will help you relax your mind, reduce anxiety and stress, enhance your capacity to concentrate, and improve your ability to make decisions.

Feel your body, bring your attention to it, take some deep breaths, and focus on the sensation of air entering into you while you do so. Do this whenever you find yourself having negative thoughts, whether they come to you consciously or unconsciously. Pay close attention to the feeling in your arms, your feet, and the rest of your body as a whole.

And all of a sudden, the pessimistic thought vanishes. It's not there anymore. You may have prevailed in this engagement, but you must now prepare for the war. That is, if you desire tranquility. That's what everyone says, right? I hope you have a wonderful day and that you are able to appreciate the priceless journey that is meditation. Peace.

COMPARE YOURSELF ONLY WITH YESTERDAY'S VERSION OF YOURSELF

Comparing yourself to others becomes second nature for most of us from an early age. It is something that happens so frequently that we do it almost unconsciously and unconsciously, and it is an inclination of our conduct that does not actually add anything positive to our lives or to our levels of happiness.

You were the only student in your class who didn't have a toy, so you begged your parents to get you one every chance you got. You had to be just like them and have the same things that they did; otherwise, you would experience a different sensation. Wow... different! It's such a burden to stand out from the crowd, isn't it? That is what we have believed our entire lives, or more accurately, that is what we have been led to believe.

They put you in a math reinforcement class if you were good at literature and languages but not very good at math. This was done so that you would have the same level as the other students and so that you would not differentiate yourself from the other students. That, however, is nonsensical when viewed through the lens of my perspective. No matter how much someone tries to be like someone else, they will never be the same. There are a variety of forms of intelligence, and since the vast majority of us only possess some kind of intelligence in one area or another rather than all forms, this highlights the fact that we are all unique. Then why put forth so much effort to appear the same as everyone else? It is the most efficient way to lose your identity and stifle creativity, to make you forget the talent and skill that life gave you in one field or another. It is also the most effective way to make you forget the talent and skill that you have in one field or another.

If someone is weak in mathematics but strong in literary, don't put him in a tutoring class for mathematics but do put him in a tutoring class for literature! Because of this, he will be the only one who can fully realize his potential in the area that sets him apart from other people. If we put on an act to appear like other people, we run the risk of gaining what they have, and if we do receive what they had, do you believe it will complete you? If so, was that what you wanted to get or what the person you wanted to look like wanted?

If you act like someone you are not, you will attract things that are not compatible with who you are. You are more likely to attract things that fit with your persona or masquerade than with who you truly are.

Since we are still young, we are motivated to integrate, to feel like we are a part of something, to receive assistance, and to interact with others. Nothing about this is negative, with the exception that we are losing our identity. Nearly all of us, without even realizing it, construct an armor that serves to shield us from the so-called "assaults" of the outside world. In order to conceal any signs of vulnerability and to avoid being an easy target, we put on an air of stoicism and callousness. It's unfortunate but true that this is true to a greater or lesser extent for everyone, to varying degrees, depending on the region, the country, and the conditions in which one was raised. It is something that is rarely spoken about, yet almost all of us do it, at least in the first world. It is a type of emotional self-preservation as well as a form of personal safety.

If you reveal how you feel, they can use it against you; if you tell too much about yourself, they will envy you and judge you, etc. If you show how you feel, they can use it against you. People even pray for forgiveness when they are crying during an event, program, or other such activity. People even pray for forgiveness when they are crying during an event, program, or other such activity. What exactly do you need forgiveness for, the fact that you are alive or that you feel? It makes me sad to think that a person would be embarrassed to express that they are feeling or "vulnerable" in any way. Cry or acknowledge your sensitivity does not make you weak; rather, it makes you powerful and real, mature and aware, and I don't see anything wrong with it. My point of view is that there is nothing wrong with expressing your sensitivity or crying. I will cry no matter who is in front of me if I'm watching a movie or documentary that has a scene that makes me feel anything, whether it's a difficult or tender scene. I don't care if it's my spouse or a whole theater full of people.

The capacity to feel separates you from a world that, at times, can be hostile and cold. Feeling is pleasant, it is beautiful, it is human. It enables you to appreciate life from other points of view and to notice the minute details that make the present great. But the most important thing, feeling sets you apart from a world that can be hostile and cold.

One of the most enriching experiences one may have is coming to terms with their unique personality, complete with all of their virtues and abilities as well as their peculiarities. After removing your armor, you will be able to see the world through your actual eyes, and you will be able to attract what is suitable for your authentic self as opposed to what is suitable for your shell.

Believe it or not, we are all weirdos, and we are all just as different from one another as we are similar to one another. What exactly is the obsession of this world with having us behaving normally? If you spend your time and effort trying to be like other people, you will forget who you are. If you waste your life comparing yourself to other people, you will not be able to appreciate how much you have grown and how much you have learned along the way. If you spend your life comparing yourself to other people, you will not be able to appreciate how much you have evolved and how much you have learned along the way.

"Confronting panic is pointless; there is no competition; the only person you have to worry about is your interpretation of yesterday".

Indian Wolf

In addition to this, one of the most efficient methods to stop happiness from taking root in your life is to constantly compare yourself to other people. Because you'll be thinking about what that other person has that you don't, but they got it in a different way, and it probably means something completely different to them than it does to you. This is because you'll be comparing what you have to what they have. We are unique and cannot be compared to anyone else for the simple reason that no one else is like us. We did not receive the same upbringing or have the same parents, the same DNA, the same mentality, or the same way of viewing or carrying out things because we were not born or reared according to their standards. Why then would I want what that other person has, whether out of avarice or envy?

If that's what it takes for me to become someone else, so be it! However, you should strive to be a better version of yourself rather than imitating someone else's version of themselves.

Accept the parts of yourself that you can't alter and work to improve the aspects of yourself that you can. And whatever it is about yourself that you admire, cultivate it, enhance it, broaden it, and make it your signature and your personal stamp. If you compare yourself to another person, you should do it in order to gain something positive from the experience rather than in order to feel envious of them or to feel awful about the way things are currently going for you.

"Just be who you are. The remaining parts have already been cast in their respective roles".

Oscar Wilde

Because of my own experiences, I am certain that if one simply focuses on being themselves, their relationships will be more genuine, their friends will be more devoted and affectionate, and their overall quality of life will improve significantly.

A terrible fate awaits the person who conflates their disguise with their genuine identity, their thinking with their own selves, and their ego with their very being. We are, we do not believe we are. Obviously, if I want to be one way or another and I do what is required, I will eventually end up being that way; however, that is not what I want to express right now. Rather, I want to say something else. That we are more feeling than thinking, more being and giving than having, more in the now than in the past or the future, more present and alert rather than distracted and absent is what I mean.

Exercise:

The previous exercise, which is described in the chapter titled "Criticism and Complaint," is extremely comparable to this one. When you become aware that you are mentally or vocally comparing yourself to another person, you should immediately stop doing so. Examine yourself carefully. Consider the motivation behind this perspective you have.

Perhaps it's envy, jealousy, or even just plain old annoyance. Nothing about it is encouraging. Take a moment to pause and just breathe. Take a look over your life and everything you've accomplished up to this point to realize how far you've come. You have a place to live, food, friends, and your health, in addition to probably a great deal more... yet even with all of that, it is still more than the majority of our human brothers and sisters on the earth have.

And are we going to be the kind of people that fail to appreciate what they have? No. You must categorically refuse to allow yourself to be led astray by those thoughts, which cannot possibly bring you any benefit. Simply by virtue of the fact that you were brought into this world, you have already achieved success. You were selected from among hundreds of millions, and you traveled all the way to the egg, where you laid your first egg, gave it life, and eventually hatched.

You are great. You are wonderful no matter who you are. I want you to repeat after me, "I AM GREAT." One more time, please repeat that phrase for me: "I AM GREAT." Now with even more fervor, repeat after me: "I AM GREAT." Now get out there and achieve your goals. You own everything in this world.

COMPLAINTS AND CRITICISMS

"What a day it is!" "stupid what are you doing?" "that guy is a..." "I don't want to go to work". "I have to do that and I can't stand it". "I hate my job, but that's the way it is"... etc, etc, etc.

These comments and complaints, along with hundreds, or rather thousands of other criticisms and complaints, are what we are accustomed to hearing or saying day after day after day. They are louder and with worse terms. In point of fact, there are well-known phrases and sayings that, for some inexplicable reason, contain more than one unfavorable word or phrase but are nonetheless ingrained in our culture.

They are a complete and total waste of time and effort. Literally.

If I spend even a small portion of my time remembering how much I dislike my job, I will feel bad just for saying it, and I will feel this way from the moment I say it until the moment I leave the office or my job and stop working. If I spend even a small portion of my time remembering how much I dislike my job, I will feel bad just for saying it. And all the while, a mental recall will have been established in us that tells us things like, "I don't like this," "that sucks," and "why am I not able to find something else?" as well as other expressions that are arrogant, self-pitying, and emotionally destructive.

There are methods and means to deal with it, or more specifically, there are two ways to act: either accept it or alter it. While it is true that it is normal to be troubled by something or many things in our everyday lives, there are ways and means to deal with it.

Why should I give something that I can't change and that I already know I don't like more time in my life if I already know that I don't like it? Why should we make our disapproval known through words? That will not alleviate our unease in any way, and instead will make the situation much more difficult to deal with. It will make the job much longer and more taxing, the hours will seem to stretch on forever, and the ticking of the clock will move even more slowly than it normally does.

It may appear as though we are letting off steam and relieving ballast, but in my opinion, what we are actually doing is reinforcing and consolidating that unpleasant feeling, giving it power over us, and so negatively affecting our energy, vitality, and positivity.

Because what we express to the world through words has the potential to have either a positive or bad effect on us, we must take into account the power of the words we choose to use. Let us not keep in our lives something that does not contribute to a positive state of mind for any longer than is strictly essential. We deserve better. You deserve better.

Still to this day, when I find myself in the midst of a complaint, instead of using a disqualifying or insulting adjective that is full of anger and in which we will invest a portion of our time and energy that we will never get back, I shut up in the middle of the sentence or end it with "I don't like it." This is because I know that if I say the qualifying adjective, it will be unpleasant, and I want to avoid saying it.

We are slowly but surely indoctrinating our subconscious mind to the point where it is beginning to comprehend that we do not enjoy hearing complaints and criticisms, that they are pointless, and that we are not going to devote another second of our lives to them. By doing so, we will be in a position to put a stop to the never-ending stream of negativity that has the potential to emerge from our minds unknowingly and on its own.

Exercise:

When you become aware that you are about to lodge a complaint or offer destructive criticism, put a halt to your train of thought and refrain from speaking. Analyze it. Examine yourself carefully. Do not pass judgment, do not speak in a critical manner, and do not give the "evil" that has already occurred any authority over you. Sing, hum, dance, perform push-ups, or just chat about the things you need to get done today. Attempt to change topic. Switch gears and think about something completely different. You shouldn't give that bad mood any ground to grow on in your day.

And if you've already spoken that complaint, criticism, or harsh phrase, it's best to shift the subject and direct your attention elsewhere. You shouldn't focus on it, and you shouldn't try to improve it. Because in the end, you will be the one to foot the bill for the consequences, even if the negative event that occurred was not your fault. And despite the fact that you may not think it or believe it, the choice will have been yours nonetheless.

Although you have very little control over what goes on around you, you do have complete agency over how such occurrences "make you feel." Because you are the one who makes the choice to experience those emotions. Because of this, I no longer use phrases such as "that concerns me," "you make me uneasy," etc. in my everyday conversation. Because I am the one who gets irritated, because I am the one who gets nervous, because I am the one who, unconsciously, lets myself be carried away by that impulse and decides, automatically or not, to surrender to that torrent of emotions and hormones that makes me feel strong after anger, secure after criticism, and powerful after the rejection of the unknown. Because I am the one who gets annoyed, because I am the one who gets nervous, because I am the one who, unconsciously, lets myself be carried away.

"A disciple arrived to Socrates' home in a state of great agitation and yelled at him: Master! I feel obligated to share with you how one of your close friends recently badmouthed you.

Which, in response, Socrates retorted hastily: wait! Have you already processed through all three of these filters what it is that you intend to say to me?

The student was taken aback and enquired whether all three filters were being used.

Yes -Socrates's reply indicated- the first filter is TRUTH. The first filter is the reality of the situation. Do you have absolute certainty that what you are going to tell me is truthful from the very beginning to the very end?

The disciple gave a negative response, saying: No, I heard that from some neighbors.

If you do this, at the very least you will have applied the second filter, which is KINDNESS. Tell me, is what you want to tell me anything good that I should listen to?

Not at all; in fact, the whole opposite is true.

Ah -Socrates shouted- then let's have a look at the very last filter. Do I really need to know about it from you?

To tell you the truth, it's not actually required at all -the pupil gave their response.

The master grinned and said: Then, if it is neither true nor good nor necessary, let's put it to rest in obscurity".

History of the Socrates triple filter

This is the response that we should have when determining whether or not to let a complaint or criticism about someone or something escape our lips and resonate in our being, modifying the vibration of the complaint or critique and affecting us in a negative or good way.

If we are going to criticize or complain about something, let us first ask ourselves the following questions: is it true, is it good, and is it necessary?

The vast majority of the time, if not always, damaging criticism, insults, complaints, or victimhood are not true, nor are they good, nor are they required.

Increase the amount of love you have for yourself, and make sure the only words you tell yourself are positive ones that will inspire and urge you to be happier right now. Make the most of the power that your words provide you, and refuse to let unfavorable thoughts, feelings, or experiences alter the way you look at things or lessen the likelihood that you will have a better life.

"Be careful not to allow your scars transform you into someone you're not."

Manuscript by Paulo Coelho discovered in Accra in the year 2012

AWARENESS OF UNCONSCIOUSNESS

Certain activities become second nature to us and we carry them out without thinking. They are responses or impulses that occur underneath our conscious awareness, and they do not require our authorization to alter our conduct. They wait in a hidden part of our minds for the right opportunity to surface, which results in a response that isn't always the one we were anticipating having.

It takes time to modify an unconscious reaction because it is part of the automatic training that we have received throughout our lives. This means that changing an unconscious reaction might be difficult. It is deeply ingrained in our consciousness, and as a result, we have been conditioned to respond in a particular way. This conditioning has been so effective, in fact, that we already believe the response to be an integral part of our being.

People are creatures of habit, and it is far more difficult to break an established pattern than it is to form a new one. It is also a lot easier to form a habit in the first place. It is for this reason that in the process of learning, it is always more vital to unlearn than it is to really gain new information. However, at the same time it is also more difficult to understand.

It is challenging to alter our ideas and beliefs when those ideals and beliefs are based on something that has been established in us for a significant amount of time. because we are required to confront ourselves and dismantle an entire structured system that contributes to the formation of our identity.

But the person that adopted those beliefs yesterday is not the same person that we are today. Even if we will be pretty similar to one another, we will not be the same as we will be tomorrow. As a result, anything that we thought was helpful or valid the day before would not necessarily apply to us now.

This may provide us with sufficient cause to examine some of our behaviors, such as asking ourselves, "Do I want to remain the same person I was yesterday, who failed in certain situations, or do I want to continue living my life exactly as I am right now in the present for the rest of my life?" Or would I rather learn everything there is to know about myself through trial and error so that I can be the best version of myself tomorrow?

"The best way to forecast the future is to create it."

Abraham Lincoln

To construct a strong and reliable happiness for the future, we need to work on it today, appreciate the circumstances we find ourselves in, and have an attitude of thankfulness. If we want to have a better physique in the future, we need to be in shape now by working out and eating right, and we can't let our bad habits become routine. And this goes on.

If there is something about the outer world that we don't like, we should first investigate the reasons behind our feelings. It is absolutely reasonable to feel outraged about something, at least to some degree, if it is something that is unfair or if we watch someone being mistreated.

But if it's something more subjective, like the way your partner acts, or the multiple messages from someone who needs your help, or the way a car crosses your lane without posing a great risk to your safety, and yet you still get angry or curse, yell, or stay with discomfort inside, there's something inside you that you can improve today for your future well-being that you can work on.

We don't start asking ourselves particular questions until we become conscious of the detrimental impacts that certain unconscious habits have had, both in our own lives and in the lives of people around us, and it's only then that we begin to investigate those effects. You are free to answer them in this space as an exercise if you so choose.

Exercise:

Shouldn't I make an effort to modify my behavior if I know that it causes others or myself to be negatively affected?

Is this an inappropriate response on my part? Why do I respond in this manner?

Is it impatience, the fact that I want everything to be done the way I want it, or the need to have complete control over everything?

These kinds of inquiries might be really helpful if what we actually want to do is get rid of an undesirable habit or routine. In this way, if we experience negative emotions like as anger or depression, we will be able to turn inward to determine the source of the problem.

Because, in my opinion, when something "bothers you," it is not that something that is the reason for your anger, but rather it is you who are upset because of how you perceive the situation. This is the case because when something "bothers you," it is not that something that is the reason for your anger. You, not the purported issue, are the one who needs to change in order to find a solution to the problem.

You have no idea how many pointless fights you could prevent if you only paid attention to the fact that an impulsive reaction was going to come out of you at that moment. Then you refuse to give in to it, you investigate your emotions or thoughts, and you come to the conclusion that the issue is not the problem itself, but rather how you interpret the situation.

And believe me when I say that each one of us has at least one private issue that has to be resolved; in the perspective of those who aren't accustomed to dealing with our own brand of oddity, we are all strange.

There is no such thing as normalcy. Normalcy does not exist. At the very least, I have the impression that it is a legend. I believe that the core issue is the aspiration to be normal or the act of appearing to be normal when, deep down inside, you are aware that by doing so, you are denying who you truly are.

Be odd. Be true to yourself. Nothing to lose, nothing to gain, yet without a filter. Jump for pleasure. Shout your happiness. Run. Don't expect anything in return for your generosity. Consume something delicious. Laugh out loud. You should give someone a call that you haven't seen in a while and let them know that you've been missing them. It's important to express your regret, gratitude, and affection for one another more frequently.

And never stop being grateful for the incredible good fortune of having siblings who are still alive and well.

But I digress; let's get back to the issue at hand. We desire to change a negative aspect of ourselves, one that is detrimental to both ourselves and those in our immediate environment. You have already made significant progress if you have recognized this behavior, emotion, or unconscious impulse that you have been having. To confront oneself and one's flaws in order to create a more improved version of oneself is a feat that can only be accomplished by fearless humans. It can be difficult to confront the mental structure that you have relied on for the entirety of your life in order to function. But believe me when I say that nothing but positive outcomes can possibly result from it. The real magic happens when you step outside of your comfort zone and into the zone of "positive discomfort." It is the place where you will experience the greatest growth, where you will flow freely and with ease, and where you will discover who you are.

It's kind of weird that in order to truly feel at peace, you have to go through some form of discomfort first, but I don't think the idea is so foreign or novel to us. For instance, we get a sense of satisfaction after completing a strenuous workout, bringing an extended project to a successful conclusion after working on it for months, or quitting smoking after struggling to do so for a number of years. It is a flash of insight in which we are totally conscious and in the here and now, concentrating all of our energy on the experience of being fully present in the here and now. After a lot of hard work and making some sacrifices, we have finally accomplished something truly remarkable. And how lovely it feels, doesn't it? After achieving anything that required a lot of hard work, there is a tremendous sense of accomplishment, happiness, and relief that comes with it. After enduring a lengthy period of "discomfort," we were finally able to realize a significant objective; however, the sacrifice of that "discomfort" in exchange for a turning point in our life was well worth it. And all of this is possible because you are here, in the moment, fully concentrated, and fully focused on the here and now. Accomplishing amazing things one baby step at a time. Let us cherish and comprehend the genuine power of being more conscious in our lives and being constructively "uncomfortable." This will allow us to live our lives more intentionally.

Exercise:

Consider whether aspects of yourself, such as your actions or reactions, are driven by impulse or unconsciousness and have a detrimental impact on you or the people around you.

Stop talking as soon as you become aware that you have spoken anything that you did not intend to say. Examine your own actions. Take two long, leisurely breaths in and out. Please answer the following questions on the piece of paper in front of you: Why did I say or do that?

What was he hoping to accomplish by making that statement or taking those actions?

What do you think, was I successful? Was it really worth it to react in such a manner?

If you have answered the questions in an honest manner, you will be able to examine what occurred from a new angle. Examine the ostensible impetus for your decision to respond in the manner that you did. Is it genuine, or is it just the way you perceive it that causes you to react in such a manner? If we go inward when we sense that something is off, we can realize that the most of the time the issue was not on the outside, but rather in the way that we interpreted what we saw on the outside.

Don't be upset with the person you are right now. You can speed up the healing process and boost your motivation by saying out loud what it is that you would like to hear, accepting yourself, and taking care of yourself. You responded in accordance with the level of consciousness you possessed at that that moment, and that is all there is to it.

The only way to take control of your life and make it your own is to cultivate consciousness. When you are conscious, you are the one who draws your life; when you are not conscious, your life is the one who draws you.

"The subconscious will govern your life until the unconscious becomes conscious, and you will call what it does fate until then".

Carl Gustav Jung

To begin with, we have to accept the fact that there is at least one aspect of ourselves that possesses room for growth. An imperfection, a negative attitude, or anything else that does not add anything positive to the quality of our lives. From that point forward, we are able to separate the behavior or reaction in question from ourselves and get insight into what is going on. Even though we won't have completed the task just yet, at least we'll have gotten it off the ground. By doing so, we will create a kind of mental mark that will allow us to recognize that reaction the next time it occurs, which will allow us to avoid missing it. Because of this, we will be able to forestall the development of an attitude, action, or mood that is excessive compared to what is required. Because when it occurs, we will be able to recognize that this conduct does not belong to us, and we will be able to revert to a mental attitude that is either positive or neutral.

And so, as time goes on, this reaction will be limited until it reaches a point where it no longer occurs, because consciously, we have been positively programming the unconscious, making it understand that we do not like this reaction because it does not take us anywhere and is of no use to us. And so, as time goes on, this reaction will be limited little by little until it reaches a point where it no longer occurs. There will come a time when we will realize that our immediate response to particular occurrences is not the same as it was many months or even several years before.

It is a process that involves perseverance, awareness, and patience; nonetheless, the end result will be well worth the effort and will significantly improve the quality of our lives.

PLEASURE FOR PLEASURE'S SAKE

How incredibly tasty the cuisine is, and how much we look forward to the sweets. Or how much we enjoy having satisfying sexual encounters; how much we enjoy smoking; how much we enjoy going shopping; how much we enjoy making and spending money. Or how enjoyable it is to have a beer while sitting on a terrace in the middle of the summer.

The vast majority of these products or activities are not in any way detrimental. In point of fact, occasionally "indulging" in the "luxury" of having a few drinks while chatting with friends or going shopping to feel lovely is not only recommended but also considered to be healthy.

Nobody is going to take care of you as well as you do, so don't expect anyone else to. It is quite beneficial to indulge in self-care and make time for quiet reflection and relaxation; in fact, we should do this not just as a reward for our efforts but also just for the sheer pleasure of it. Because our purpose in this life is not only to work and work, worry and worry about our duties and bills, and pay the bills that we owe. It is necessary to pull the train over at random intervals, disembark, breathe in some clean air, and experience the gentle warmth of the sun on your face. Try to feel more and think less. However, that is not the central point at all.

When I talk about pleasure just for the sake of pleasure, I mean basing your happiness solely on the ability to experience pleasurable things. That is, thinking that you are happy because you have more money, more sex, or because you feel superior to someone else, or because you have spent it on frivolous items or indulgences; or because you have earned more money... That is the genuine error, and in point of fact, it is a genuine accusation.

Because there will come a time when you will have done everything, or almost everything, and you will feel empty, unsatisfied, depressed, and irascible, and you will take it out on yourself or your loved ones, and you will try to drown your sorrows in alcohol, overeating, drugs, sex, etc...... Because there will come a time when you will have done everything, or almost everything, and you will feel empty, unsatisfied, depressed And with that, we are back where we started.

"The search for pleasure inevitably results in suffering".

Herodotus

One of my close friends is worth a million dollars. And fortunately, he is the kind of person who is optimistic, grateful, and happy. However, he reveals to me that many of his pals, who are also millionaires, are either addicted to cocaine, sex, alcohol, or prostitution; are lonely and depressed; or are prostitutes.

This is due to the fact that they have pleasure and happiness mixed up in their minds. It can be summed up in a single sentence, but the concept behind it may be difficult to grasp. I will make an effort to describe it in a more understandable manner: It is an external stimulation that provides us a pleasant feeling of well-being, a source of hormones that flood our organism and revolutionize it. Pleasure originates from the outside; it is a stimulus that arrives from the outside. Whether it be from the consumption of unhealthy foods that contain flavor enhancers, processed sugar, and other artificial additives, or whether it be from the acquisition of wealth, narcotics, political power, or sexual activity. The feeling of pleasure is not something that can be sustained. It arrives, it energizes us, and then it fades away, leaving behind only a hazy recollection of how wonderful it was while it lasted. After that, we require another dose in order to satisfy our parched throats. It's a tale that goes on forever.

"Because it is a number, money is something that will never run out. If you believe that money can bring you satisfaction, then your quest for happiness will never be satisfied".

Bob Marley

Happiness, on the other hand, is an internal state that can't be manufactured. It is a state of mind as well as a way of life. It's not about where you end up so much as how you get there. Even if it may be pouring rain outside, the interior of the building may have the feel of a pleasant and sunny day. We do not require anything physical in order to experience joy; rather, it is the lens through which we view the world that determines our level of contentment. You don't have to sit around and wait for the storm to pass; instead, you should learn how to move gracefully in the water.

People often suggest that gratefulness is a trait shared by joyful people, but I don't see it that way. My theory is that happy individuals are those who are grateful for what they have. Because if we place importance on what we have, how we feel, and who we are, everything else in our environment will take on a different hue. When they change our work schedule, we will focus on what we can do by having a different shift, like that pending task we wanted to do; or if we have to work more, we can think that we will earn more money if we work more hours and what we can invest it in, etc. A rainy day will look nice because we will be at home warm or in good company; or when they change our work schedule, we will focus on what we can do by having a different shift, etc.

"It has been said that "half of the beauty depends on the landscape, and the other half depends on the individual who looks at it".

Lin Yutang

As was covered in the section titled *"Being grateful makes you happy"*, if we are conscious of the plenty that is all around us and the privileges that we possess, we will, of course, experience an extraordinary amount of happiness.

When I mentioned that happiness comes from within and pleasure comes from the outside, I was referring to this same concept. When we keep in mind how fortunate we are, when we value our health, our life, our friendships or family relationships, when we appreciate the love of our partner or our pet, when we enjoy a sunny or rainy day, when we are grateful to have a roof over our heads, a plate on the table, a job, good conversations or company, and a long list of other things, then we will not require an external stimulus to feel happy. Because the sense of inner calm and thankfulness that we will have will be so powerful, this experience will take our energies to a new level, and our perspective on the outside world will shift as a result. We shall each view the same sky via our own unique perspective. We are going to walk in a different order along the same trail. The world as we know it will still exist, but our species will have progressed. Suddenly, our worries will be less concerned, our issues will be less severe, our anger will lessen till it completely vanishes, and smiles will become our new language.

"If you don't change, everything will keep happening the same way".

Anonymous

Because we will have realized that the secret is not to acquire but to just be, happiness will come easily and almost unintentionally to us. This is because our focus will no longer be on material possessions. Even at those times when you don't seem to be doing well and you have a poor patch, when multiple difficulties or anxieties come together, even then, there is surely a lot to be grateful for. At the end of the day, it all comes down to being happy and making people around us happy.

Exercise: It is easy, I recommend that we write on paper everything that we know does not do us any good, neither in terms of our physical health nor our mental or emotional well-being, yet we continue to give it a place in our lives. Take it out of yourself, make it part of the world around you, and make an effort to view it in an isolated or more objective manner.

"If you are aware of what has to be done but choose not to take action, your situation will become much more dire than it was before".

Confucius

Let's give straightforward responses to these questions:

What am I getting out of this poor habit or this excessive amount?

Doing it gives me joy, but does it also make me happier? Does it also make me a better person?

If I stopped doing it, what do you think would happen?

How can I receive the same sensation that you provide me through means that are safer and more natural, or how can I acquire a sensation that is even better for my health and that lasts for a longer period of time?

If that's the case, then why don't I go with that option?

It is not my place to pass judgment on you. I have been there, and it is my intention to walk you through the steps that I took that were successful for me in order to stop being a slave to the mind, the negative impulses, and the unconsciousness that governs almost all of us to a great extent. I have been there, and it is my intention to show you the steps that I followed that worked for me.

Nobody but you will see your responses, so it is important that you strive to be as truthful as you possibly can. This will allow you to identify the source of the 'issue' as quickly as possible, which is not a problem at all but rather an essential fact brought on by distraction or unconsciousness.

You may also choose to discuss this information with your significant other or other loved ones, who may be able to assist you in the search for tangible evidence, so making the process simpler and more pleasurable for you.

It is very vital that we take some time out of our lives to relieve ourselves of the weight that we believe we have to bear alone and communicate how we are feeling to the people who are closest to us. In this way, we are able to externalize the "issue," and by doing so, everything becomes relativized and, to some extent, loses its significance.

Let go of any feelings of shame, pride, or fear, and bring out whatever it is that is hiding inside you that is preventing you from moving forward.

It is a very healthy thing to do, and something that might be beneficial for everyone, to empty your backpack of stones. In addition to this, you will realize that it's possible that you shouldn't have acquired so many of them, and as a result, you may rethink your decision to do so in the future.

CHOOSE WISELY THE BATTLES TO FIGHT

There are a lot of different ways that something could be misunderstood, and there are a lot of different possibilities: perhaps I was unable to explain myself as I wanted to, perhaps I choose the incorrect words or tone, or perhaps the time, the looks, or the body expression were all off. In addition, whether you receive this message by means of a phone call, an email, a text message on your mobile phone, etc. That is to say, if they read it, all they have to do is picture how I would have stated it and interpret it in their own way.

It's possible that the other person was having a difficult day, felt bad, and lacked the patience to pause and think about whether the comments meant one thing or another at the time. And because of the way your mind is built as well as the knowledge you gained as you were growing up, it will also help you interpret it in either the positive or negative sense.

It seems like it would be simpler than it actually is to come to a disagreement or misunderstanding based on perceived differences, doesn't it? Why, therefore, do you care to be right? It's possible that none of them is right, or perhaps both! Everyone read the words in their own manner, and even though there was no malice intended on either side, a ridiculous misunderstanding may have been reached as a result. This makes it extremely relative and subjective.

There are numerous methods to know how to choose our "battles," or, more accurately, to avoid duels of egos that lead nowhere; nonetheless, I base myself totally on Buddhist knowledge in this instance, as I do in many others.

- Free yourself from the need to feel offended

It is not the words of the other person that cause you to feel offended; rather, it is the expression or attitude of the other person that causes you to feel offended. You are the one who "decides," whether consciously or unconsciously, to feel offended or angry. You are easily upset by even the most innocuous things. Because you disagree with it, because it goes against your principles, because it's not the way you would do it or the way you want to see it, and because it conflicts with your ideas.

Do not put up a fight, and do not allow the notion to provoke an unneeded and possibly unjustifiable response from you. Accept it and then ask yourself whether it really is as you perceive it or whether there is even the tiniest chance that it could be something else entirely while still being completely accurate.

Do not make it personal, focus on taking care of yourself, and work toward achieving inner peace. It is obvious that you should take action whenever you can in order to prevent injustice and abuse.

Because by taking offense, you are concentrating and intensifying the negative energy that already exists within you, so causing it to persist for a longer period of time.

- Free yourself from the need to succeed in everything you do:

"Everyone discusses peace, but no one actually teaches about how to achieve it. Education is given to people in *order to compete, and competitiveness is the root cause of all wars".*

Lipnisky

What some people perceive as "losing," other people view as an opportunity to grow. What some people consider to be "winning," other people refer it as "enjoying." If you let the desire to win affect you or transform you in any way, you will become someone cold and apathetic who only seeks victories and titles to puff up his chest and boast of a beautifully adorned identity, but who is empty on the inside. If you don't let it affect you or transform you, you will remain the same person who wants to win because it is a way for the ego to feel powerful.

We've all been on the receiving end of victories and defeats, but does it make a difference in how you view the world? In point of fact, it's possible that failing to succeed is even more beneficial than succeeding, given that failing leaves you with a pleasant learning experience that you can cultivate, provided that you acknowledge that you are capable of learning something, provided that you are willing, and provided that you are humble. But victory does nothing but stoke the flames of ego and set you apart from other people. Who cares if the victor of today also loses tomorrow if they've already won today? Will he be depressed, irritated, and have a diminished sense of self? It doesn't make any sense. You are not defined by what you own, but rather by what you accomplish, how you feel and how others cause you to feel. You are not defined by whether you win or lose; all you need to do is try to observe without passing judgment and enjoy life without seeking to outdo anyone else but your version of yesterday.

- Let go of the desire to always prove that you are correct:

When we are listening to someone, the vast majority of the time, we are actually preparing our response, we are stockpiling ammunition to spew our reasons or motives, and we are attempting to establish that our argument is the correct and sufficient one. This is how we protect the identity we have assumed for ourselves and express our desire to set ourselves apart from other people. However, we are already distinct from one another. And the same goes for that. We are equally distinct from one another.

But we are striving for accuracy. We want to demonstrate that we are more knowledgeable and superior. But this never-ending battle is really ridiculous! I am reminded once more that none of us are experts in practically anything, but we are all students of everything. We all have a passing familiarity with several topics, but our knowledge of the others ranges from scant to nonexistent.

"You never say anything new; all you do is reiterate what other people have told you. But if you pay attention, you might pick up some useful information".

Dalai Lama

By listening without thinking about how to respond, or, more accurately, by listening without thinking at all and simply sensing the words, attitude, and knowledge that the other person is projecting, we are allowing them to contribute to us, allowing some of the knowledge that they have gained from their experiences to enter us and enrich us. The variety of life is what makes it so interesting. And within the complexities of difference is the process of evolution.

I feel a surge of freedom as soon as I let go of the ego's limiting ideas and accept the possibility that there may be other truths except the one I hold. I grow. I enable a new stream of ideas to enter my life and incorporate them into it, which makes my life more vibrant and rich. Do not shut yourself off from the flow of information that travels around the earth beyond your head, and give yourself permission to question even your own identity on occasion so that you can make room for other realities to coexist with you and interact with you.

- o Let go of the compulsion to always prove that you are better than others:

We are accustomed to, or rather addicted to, thinking that we are better than other people. It's possible that this is the root cause of so much pointless criticism, jealousy, and disdain directed against people who have more or less than us, those who are different from us, and those who are similar to us. It makes no difference; the important thing is that you feel powerful. By looking down on other people, I can avoid facing my anxieties, flaws, and insecurities, which are the factors that lead me to search for my strength in impolite speech and behavior, in expensive vehicles and clothes, in jewelry, and in other empty vices.

We both hail from the same region, thus it only seems sense that we should run into each other there.

You only need to be better than you were the day before; you just need to be a better version of yourself. That is the only person you have to fight against in order to achieve your goal of winning. Period.

- Set yourself free from the desire to accumulate more things:

To possess, to possess, to possess. to gratify our appetites, our egos, and our desires to feel superior to others or to be included in a group. There are more beneficial methods to feel integrated into a group than simply possessing everything that everyone else has. If you are a one-night stand, you will never have enough. If you are consumed with vices and pleasures, you will eventually burn out and lose your meaning and reason for being along the way. If you love money, you will always want more of it. If you are a one-night stand, you will never have enough.

If you achieve one of your goals, you will immediately start planning for the next one, and you will end up wasting precious time that could be spent living, loving, and learning instead of focusing on the next title or trophy to add to your collection.

The pursuit of happiness, rather than achieving it, is the real prize. It is more important to be than to have.

These are the principles of Buddhism that we will cover today; however, there are many others that are just as interesting.

If we are unable to appreciate what we already have, acquiring more things will not bring us happiness; therefore, learning to not feel offended, forgetting our false need to be right, winning, or feeling superior, and accepting that having more will not bring us freedom are all necessary steps toward achieving this goal. Free from the sway of our ego, free from the unconscious urges that do us no good, and free to know how to pick and select our conflicts effectively.

Have fun while you're learning these new skills, and make sure to put them to good use so you can keep your calm.

"If you want to see change in the world, you have to be the change".

Mahatma Gandhi

In this section, please list the ideas that have most intrigued you up to this point:

_____
_____

In what ways do you intend to put these ideas into practice in your daily life?

_____
_____

After you have finished writing these lines, you should read them out loud so that you can start to internalize them.

HIGH VIBRATION

"If you want to find out the mysteries of the cosmos, you need to think about energy, frequency, and vibration".

Nicola Tesla

According to the fundamental principles of quantum physics, there is a constant transfer of energy happening between our bodies and the surrounding world. Therefore, we had better make sure that what surrounds us is good and positive in order for the energy that reaches us to be enriching and useful, and also so that we do not run out of energy to use in our own development and evolution. If we do not take this precaution, we will run the risk of running out of energy.

How many times have you just chatted to a wonderful friend and you feel great, just brimming with enthusiasm, thankfulness, and vitality? How often does this happen to you? This is not a random occurrence. It's more of a causal relationship. Or, think back to the other times when you've just finished a conversation with someone who is always negative, always criticizing others, always envying, insulting, and belittling others at every opportunity they get, and by the time you realize it, you're exhausted, depressed, and you don't feel like doing anything. I believe that all of us have experienced something similar, but the question is whether or not we are aware of what is taking place.

There are those who give, and there are those who take away; there are those with whom you exchange energy, and there are others who leave you feeling depleted, dried out, and shriveled. On the flip side, there are other people in your life who can reinvigorate, strengthen, and motivate you. We are energy, and this fact cannot be disputed; nonetheless, it is sometimes necessary to pay attention to these particulars in order to fully comprehend the notion, as well as the force and influence that it may have on our life.

If we are energy and that energy is vibration at a certain frequency, then we could argue that the energy that makes up our bodies is either in a state of high vibration or low vibration at any given instant. Every emotion is associated with a particular vibration, the positive ones having higher frequencies and the negative ones having lower ones.

There are a lot of things that might influence our vibration, including the following:

- Environment: it's possible that more things in your immediate surroundings have an impact on you than you realize. Maintaining order and cleanliness in your house or place of business not only makes it easier to find things, but it also helps bring quiet and tranquility to your mind and soul and ensures that you are not absorbing chaotic energy from your surroundings.
- Music: when we listen to music, its vibrations and energy can instantly boost or reduce our own frequency since, like us, music is made up of vibrations and energy. When meditating or working, it can be helpful to tune into the appropriate frequency by listening to music that is happy, energetic, or 432 Hz.

- Visual stimulation: the information that is sent from the retina to the brain via the ocular nerve is deposited in our subconscious, where it plants a seed that may or may not eventually develop the desirable fruits we anticipate. We receive signals that remain in the unconscious part of our mind and tell us that we could have more and better, that what we have and what surrounds us is not the most recent, the most beautiful, the most expensive, or the youngest. This happens when we watch movies of violence, misfortunes, or news that makes you fearful and distrustful, or when we see advertising that motivates your consumerism and dissatisfaction with your current partner, house, car, or physique. It may appear to be innocuous, but after years and years of being exposed to information that is inconsistent, our minds can start to play tricks on us, and it may be difficult to determine the source of your dissatisfaction. This is especially true if the factor that is causing your dissatisfaction has been deemed acceptable, as it is something that we take in on a daily basis.
- Company: some people believe that we are a reflection of the individuals who are closest to us on average. So let's make sure we're surrounded by positive influences! We have reached the stage where we may choose our own company; thus, let's make wise choices. Being around happy, thankful, and optimistic individuals will make us feel better and bring more positive experiences into our lives. Negative people, on the other hand, who live their lives in a state of perpetual complaint and criticism and who constantly victimize each other will not

assist us in attracting anything positive into our lives and will only serve to attract more negative experiences. Make judicious decisions.

- Words: We should never, ever, undervalue the tremendous power that words possess. Just as anything said to us can make us happy, sad, or angry, the words we choose to say to others have the power to either boost them up or bring them down. Words bring with them a potent charge of identity and intention that has the potential to move mountains and puts every cell in our body to work with the energy that we receive. Because of this, many times we experience negative emotions simply by picturing something that has not even taken place. This is due to the fact that the mind and the spoken word have a powerful influence over our life. Because of this very reason, I have been known to repeat over and over again that criticism and destructive complaints are pointless. This is due to the fact that, even if the person or the fact in question is deserving of criticism, some of those negative words will splash us and contaminate our energy, resulting in a decrease in our vitality, positivity, and overall effectiveness.

"There is not yet a calming medication developed by modern technology that is as beneficial as a few words of kindness".

Sigmund Freud

- Thoughts: finally, but certainly not least, we come to our ideas. The beginning of everything else. The basic material from which our most pleasant dreams or our worst nightmares might be materialized and experienced.

- o The crucial endeavor of "taking care" of our ideas is discussed in a variety of various ways across the several chapters contained in this book. Some of these include *"An objective reading of the situation"*, *"Awareness of the unconsciousness"*, *"How to be positive?"* and *"Try to feel more and think less."*

The human brain is a constant source of electrical impulses, which we refer to as thoughts. And if everything in the cosmos is energy, just think about what happens to those things. They go out into the cosmos as a vibration with a frequency, and then they return to you in the shape of facts or justifications for you to continue thinking that way. It's a little bit like the mirror effect, or like dropping a pebble into a body of water. The stone (or thought) will generate ripples that will spread out in all directions around the surrounding 360 degrees. These ripples will be infinitesimally smaller and undetectable to humans, but they will continue until they have completed their journey. And sooner or later, they will ricochet back to the source, which can be either our thoughts or our existence, manifested in the language (high or low vibration) that they were released in.

To put it succinctly, if you have negative ideas and give an excessive amount of attention to those negative thoughts on a regular basis, you will attract additional reasons, facts, and feelings into your life that will enable you to remain in that negative vibration. If, on the other hand, you make the decision to let go of those negative thoughts and focus your attention solely on the positive ones, practicing mindfulness and making an effort to live in the present moment with gratitude and love, then positive occurrences in your life will serve to validate the validity of that thought. It may appear to be a theory or an impossibility, but I can attest to the fact that it is effective, and besides, what have you got to lose by giving it a shot?

BALANCE

There is a hierarchy that rules over everything that exists on this planet. There are moments when it appears to be disordered, sometimes it appears to be senseless or chaotic, but in the end, there is an order. Everything must operate in accordance with a specific functionality, and if there is ever a disruption in this equilibrium, it will result in a chain reaction of unfavorable effects. We humans, on the other hand, have the illusion that our lives are unaffected by or subservient to this order. Until everything goes over us, we believe that we are the masters of everything and that we are above everything. We are not immune to the laws that direct the operation of this cosmos. Let us not forget that we are not merely a part of the universe; rather, we ARE the universe. The same kinds of matter and compounds that make up the stars also make up our bodies. If we are successful in altering our being, our dynamics, our attitude, and our behaviors, then our surroundings will unavoidably shift as a result.

But we fail to recognize our capacity for original thought. We live in a world that is constantly bombarded with stimuli and distractions, feelings and addictions, all of which serve to obscure our perceptions and keep us from realizing our full potential. We are the ones that create, we are the ones who are creative, and we are either all or nothing. Naturally, we are inextricably linked to our surroundings since energy connects everything, and the energy that allows us to make our goals a reality in the physical world is our thoughts. And most of the time it just pops into our heads out of nowhere, and even though we believe we have a lot of control over what it says, there are instances when we don't. Finding ways to positively affect our dreams in the real world is a necessity for us, and we must find those ways. We have to figure out a way to have a good influence on our subconscious in order to turn those negative, habitual, illogical, and counterproductive thoughts more pleasant, calmer, and more logical. In the event that this does not occur, we will continue to merely engage in an effort to completely develop both our potential and the goal or work that we came here to complete.

The only way to make something function properly is to establish order. It is the algorithm, the formula, and the recipe for the cake that your grandmother used to make.

You will be able to display all of your talent and skill on the game board once you have found your order, which will allow you to discover your equilibrium.

By order, I do not mean that your accommodation is in a convenient location, although this is also included. If, in accordance with the theory of quantum energy, energy flows from us to us and all around us, then an excessive number of items that are out of place will prevent the energy from flowing normally and will prevent us from experiencing a renewal of our vitality and creativity. Aside from that, wouldn't it be true that simply taking in how clean the space is would instantly soothe the mind? Despite the fact that we have long been accustomed to seeing something messy, the instant emotion that comes over us when we see it clean and tidy is one of serenity and restfulness, regardless of whether or not we want to see it. It is not a bad thing to have the room or the kitchen messy from time to time, especially after a meal with friends or a day of work. On the other hand, it is not healthy to be obsessed with cleanliness all day long and to suffer when you see a crumb of bread on the floor and lose your temper. Those of us who have pets are familiar with this phenomenon. Simply put, and in my opinion, making it a habit to clean up after oneself or to not create a great deal of clutter is something that is really beneficial to one's health and can be very calming. This is because it provides us with a lovely place in which to relax and recharge our energies and ideas.

In the same manner, you need to have order in your life, whether it be your routines or your activities, because this is the most effective approach to accomplish what you have set out to do and to attain your highest level of productivity throughout the day, the week, and the month...

Concerns that require your attention in order to put your life in order

There are some issues that many of us have engrained in us that act as a roadblock to our genuine progress. These issues can affect you.

In particular, I would like to call attention to the following:

Aversion to the unfamiliar: because we are "moving away" from what we are accustomed to when we make changes, we may expcrience feelings of discomfort or rejection. However, breaking out of your comfort zone is one of the most effective methods to reach your objectives and be successful, if not the only way.

A common theme that runs throughout this book is the danger of engaging in excessive levels of mental activity. One of the greatest keys to unlocking your genuine hidden potential is to reduce the amount you think and increase the amount you feel.

You should avoid thinking or saying negative things about yourself since a portion of you will eventually believe them, which will lower your energy levels, effectiveness, positivism, and chances of being successful.

"Do not speak poorly of yourself, for the warrior that resides inside you will hear your words and be diminished as a result of them".

Ancient samurai proverb

If you don't want to do something, please say so; if you don't want to go out for a drink that day, please say so; if you can't do something or don't want to do something for some reason, please don't do it. If you ensure that you are healthy and that you take care of yourself, you will be in a position to care for others without encountering any difficulties.

Putting off until tomorrow what can be done today: taking a break and doing "nothing" for a day or so is not only healthful but also highly advised. Putting off until tomorrow what can be done today: But if we let it become our routine, our way of being, and our habit, we will throw away priceless time that we will never be able to get back and that we could have used to create, learn, work, or accomplish something.

Exercise:

To kickstart the process of introducing new, beneficial behaviors into your life, you should begin by creating a calendar of events or plans. You can get started with a manageable amount, and then gradually increase it during the month so that you don't feel rushed or overwhelmed. There is no doubt that there is some activity that you would like to participate in, some book that you would like to read, and some cuisine that you would like to learn how to make.

Fill up your schedule, set goals for yourself to improve, and be open to new experiences. Because the only constant is the fact that everything is in a state of perpetual flux, and this is the one thing that will never change.

Acquire a fresh notebook, and then fill it with your ideas. Write out in large letters what it is that you wish to accomplish. Keep a page free for jotting down ideas, rough thoughts, or drafts of strategy and budgets. Create a new to-do list on a new page each day. Be specific, but don't get down on yourself or put undue stress on yourself if you don't accomplish what you set out to do. Just keep going. If you are successful in completing the majority of the items on your daily to-do list, rather than berating yourself for failing to complete all of the items on the list, you should instead take pride in the fact that you have already accomplished more than you did the day before when you did not use a list, notebook, or even a beginning point.

Keep in mind that if we want to include everyday activities in our routine, the easiest way to do so is to get started cautiously. Changes that take place gradually are preferable because they are more likely to be maintained over an extended period of time. In this way, we will not have the desire to give up.

Your software should have new tasks added every seven to fifteen days. If you want to exercise more frequently, you should begin by working out only two or three days per week and gradually increase the number of days you exercise every one to two weeks. This will allow your body and mind to become accustomed to the increased demand and prevent you from becoming discouraged and giving up.

If you bring order to your life, you will be able to better appreciate the times of leisure, rest, and even work; in addition, your productivity will increase, and the results will become obvious immediately and with weight in your day-to-day existence; and you will be able to work more efficiently.

POSITIVE DISCOMFORT

After gaining an awareness of the significance of stepping outside of one's comfort zone, this idea became deeply ingrained in my mind. Or, to put it another way, instead of sitting about waiting for the right opportunity to strike, you should seize it and make it your own.

We are well aware that we are creatures of routine, and that when we arrive home, we prefer to kick off our slippers, have a drink, eat dinner, read a book or watch a movie, depending on what we feel like doing at the time. It is a method of feeling at peace and there is nothing terrible about it, at least not when it is in the appropriate balance. We feel secure and comfortable in the pattern that habit provides.

However, if maintaining that comfy habit keeps us from working on ourselves, taking chances on new projects or creating new connections, or participating in a variety of activities in order to get a breadth of experiences, then it can't be particularly beneficial.

To a certain extent, everything is beneficial, but if we wish to develop as individuals or businesspeople, misusing the benefits of comfort can be extremely destructive to our efforts.

"If you believe that adventure is risky, try doing the same thing over and over again. It's a death sentence".

Paulo Coelho

This expression helps us see things from a different angle than the one we are typically accustomed to.

Again, it goes without saying that we all enjoy the feeling of being at ease in our own homes or with some circumstance, activity, or enterprise that we have previously mastered. The willingness to want to better, on the other hand, or the drive to reach our limit and then beyond it, is a very positive and satisfying thing to have.

We have to come to terms with the fact that the vast majority of the information we know comes from experience, and more specifically, from unpleasant situations, as this is when we learn the most.

Enjoyment and education may be found in every aspect of life; therefore, there is no reason not to put this information to good use. Let's make it a goal to fail frequently!

"If you want to succeed, double the amount of errors you make," the proverb goes.

Thomas Watson

I'm not suggesting you should fail on purpose, but you should attempt new ideas, try new projects, fail, learn, and adapt. People who have achieved a great deal of success often discuss the value of setbacks, or the "failures" that the rest of us tend to see with such contempt. However, they are not the same thing at all. They present wonderful possibilities for education, advancement, and the pursuit of one's goals. It's safe to say that nearly no one does it right the first time they attempt, so the sheer fact that you have the opportunity to do it again is a privilege. Now that we've had a moment to catch our breath, let's think about how we can make the next attempt even better and then give it our all.

Consider the following scenario as a concrete illustration of what to do when you want to go to the gym or exercise:

When we go to sleep the night before we motivate ourselves and convince ourselves that this is what we want to accomplish, we think about beginning the next day or the week to its maximum potential, and when we wake up, we say to ourselves, "I can do this!" When it comes down to it, we find a thousand and one persuasive excuses not to do it because we either get lazy, something hurts, or anything else.

"Those who want to accomplish something will find a way to do it, and those who want to do nothing will find an excuse".

Arabic proverb

It no longer appears to be a choice that can be made, but rather a duty that must be fulfilled. And when you think about it, that ruins the whole experience, doesn't it?

Even if doing something that requires little effort gives us a great deal of satisfaction and makes us feel positive and fulfilled, it is extremely challenging for us to turn off the thoughts that are running through our heads, get off the couch where we are safe, and engage in an activity that is rewarding. But I think that the act of doing something different, or moving out of our comfort zone, is what drives us to reject it in the first place. [Case in point:]

On the other hand, while we are in the middle of the workout, five to ten minutes after we begin, we have a fantastic feeling, our minds are calm and free of stress, we can feel the blood circulating throughout the body, giving it energy, and when the workout is over, we feel like winners!

Exercise:

Think about the activities that you typically complete throughout the day, but that you do so unwillingly or because you lack the enthusiasm to do so. Let's adjust that perspective and mentality for you so that you can approach them with enthusiasm and positive energy. Imagine what may happen if we did everything in this manner: if you adopt a more optimistic outlook, the environment around you will shift dramatically.

It is of the utmost importance to reassure and persuade oneself that the motivation behind our actions is pleasure, not compulsion or duty. Before we get started with the exercise, we can even affirm it aloud numerous times before we do it.

For instance, make sure you remember to say out loud things like "I want to swim," "I really like it," and "I feel fantastic." This can help you feel more satisfied and proud of yourself, in addition to boosting your health and fitness. Insist that you should say "I want to swim," rather than "I have to swim." It is important to do so frequently in order to reinforce this uplifting feeling of personal development. In this way, whenever we start to feel unmotivated about engaging in a particular activity that requires us to leave the couch or our comfort zone, we will be able to bring to mind the fact that it is beneficial for us, how good we feel while engaging in it, and how, at the end of the day, we feel proud and satisfied with the effort that we put in.

"Do something terrifying to yourself every single day".

Theodora Roosevelt, Eleanor

This has nothing to do with jumping out of an airplane while wearing a parachute. Or I am. I'm talking about being brave enough to try new things and embracing the feelings of insecurity and uncertainty that come along with venturing into uncharted territory. I'm talking about making an effort to alter one's behavior and take an alternative route. We might "fail," due to the fact that we are new in that habitat, or we might find something different that expands our eyes and provides us what we have been looking for such a long time and what we needed the most.

"Modify your actions occasionally if you want to see various outcomes from the actions you take".

Albert Einstein

If you can find your groove, you will see that becoming a better version of yourself is not only not frightening, but also one of the most exciting and fulfilling things that you can do in your life.

To be able to propose something and see it through to completion is to be able to actualize our ideas in the physical world. The intangible is made to appear more real as a result. It is a miracle. And life itself is a magical experience.

WHAT HAPPENS IF YOU AID ANOTHER PERSON?

"Just as rivers do not consume their own water, trees do not consume the fruit they bear." The flowers do not spread their scent all by themselves, just as the sun does not shine for itself. Serving other people should be second nature to everyone.

When you're happy, life is fantastic, but it's even better when you make other people happy as a result of your happiness. Serving others comes naturally to us. Whoever does not serve in order to live, does not live in order to serve".

Jorge Bergoglio

When I was younger, I overheard someone say that if everyone assisted their neighbor, nobody would require assistance. It seems to me that this tells a lot about what we are capable of accomplishing if we learn to be more empathic and sensitive, as well as if we learn to work more collectively rather than independently.

From a young age on, we were instilled with the value of competing with others in order to achieve success in academics and athletics, to acquire more desirable possessions, and so on. We spend our entire lives trying to categorize ourselves into categories that we think best describe who we are, but which, in my view, just serve to set us apart from the other individuals in our immediate environment. There is, of fact, such a thing as healthy competition; however, the reason why it is not always practiced is because we tend to concentrate more on the things that divide us than on the things that bring us together. Does the fact that a person "belongs" to something, such as a soccer team, a specific political ideology, a religion, a specific social class, a gender, or a country, make them superior to those who do not "belong" to those things? In no way, shape, or form. It only makes you different. And this is a very positive development. Take for example the natural world, which is teeming with color and variety, as well as difference and vitality. That it possesses such a varied wealth and an abundance of such a wide variety of things contributes to its overall attractiveness. Obviously, it's a good thing to stand out from the crowd. In fact, I'd go so far as to say that acknowledging the quirks and idiosyncrasies that are innate to each of us and embracing them is not only necessary but also what makes us free and powerful.

When we compare ourselves to other people and focus on the ways in which we are unique from them, we unintentionally construct invisible barriers that keep us apart from them. As a result, we begin to view our uniqueness in a pessimistic light and shut the door on our own growth, rather than being mindful of the amazing educational opportunities that are available to us.

If we simply socialize with people who are "similar" to us, we won't advance our knowledge very much. It will be a fantastic opportunity for us to extend our perspective and learn new things if we come together with people whose ages, ideologies, cultures, religions, countries, and sexes are all different from our own.

Because of our unconscious rejection of the different and the unknown, as well as our deep "love" of comfort, I feel that this is the primary issue that contributes to the fact that we do not have a natural tendency to be more open with other people. We do this automatically and frequently. And we don't have to travel very far to notice it, or to locate a case of contrasts between nations, faiths, or cultural practices. In the same nation, people living in the capital may have a different attitude toward those living in the suburbs, or those living in the suburbs may have a different attitude toward those living in the capital, or people living in a village may confront the village next door and reject each other. It is unfortunate that this still occurs in the 21st century, but it does, and the root of the problem is a fear of the unknown, a fear of not being in control of the situation, and a fear of losing our traditions or beliefs. This limits the acquisition of new knowledge, which in turn stops progress and stunts evolutionary growth.

Do not give in to the temptation of letting your mind direct your actions, and do not pay attention to it if all it can offer you is doubt or anxiety. Follow both your heart and your natural instincts; this is the part of ourselves that we have disregarded for so long but that is still there and compels us to try new things, to take risks, and to continually educate ourselves.

"The primary reason we are here in this life is to be of service to other people. And if you can't help them, at least don't make their situation any worse".

Dalai Lama

It can be summed up like that. Naturally, it's helpful even without thinking about it. And if at first we have to make an effort because it does not come easily to us, then let's compel the machine to do what we want it to do. It's all for a worthy cause, after all. To you, it might not seem like much of a difference, but to the other person, it might signify a great deal. You've already made their day or your day better, and all because of a simple gesture on your part.

And by altering yourself, you contribute to the improvement of the environment around you. It's the simple things in life that really make it all worthwhile. When combined with other "insignificant" acts, seemingly insignificant actions can have a significant impact.

There is no such thing as a minor act of kindness, and there is also no such thing as an act of kindness that goes unrewarded. It is a given that the positive energy and intention that you put out into the world will, in some form or another, find its way back to you, whether to a greater or smaller level. As a result, the cycle of humanity, which is comprised of empathy and fellowship, will run its course and will never be lost. Let us be a part of making the world a better place for others, and let us welcome only goodness and goodwill into our immediate environment. By doing things in this way, we will establish our very own world and our very own laws.

Be careful not to lose sight of the sun because of the storm. And remember to be someone's ray of sunshine today. Be the one who makes a difference, be the one who surprises and makes others doubt the injustice of the actual world, and be the one who restores hope in humanity in these modern times by being the one who makes a difference. "For no apparent reason," without a purpose or party, and without dread of divine punishment for not acting appropriately, let's spread some fantasy, joy, affection, and good manners on the ground where our human family walks. Let's do this "for no apparent reason." Let us do it because it is the right thing to do, because being kind to other people makes good things happen, and because it is an imperative need to help our equals, and by equals, I mean different, and by different, I mean equal. Let us do it because it is the right thing to do, because being kind to other people makes good things happen. Let us aid each and every individual who comes across our way, whenever we see that we can help or better their lives with a simple smile, with a kind word, with a true interest, or with a detail. Let us do this whenever we perceive that we may help or improve their lives with any of these things. It is a seed that will make the tree of humanity grow and will only bear fruits of understanding, respect, companionship, and love. No symbol of affection falls on deaf ears since it is a seed that makes the tree of humanity grow.

Exercise:

Be aware of your day-to-day life. There is someone around you whose day can be improved thanks to the help you can give them by giving them a smile, helping them push the car, or holding the door for them. Exercise: Be aware of your day-to-day life. There is someone around you who can improve their day thanks to the help you can give them. Don't let the chance pass you by to temporarily push yourself beyond of your comfort zone and assist someone else today. You will brighten that person's day, and you will have moved closer to realizing that we are all equal and equally deserving of love, respect, and opportunities in equal measure. Smile at the person you believe doesn't deserve it as much as you do, and also at the person who does. Your generosity should astound everyone you come into contact with.

In the end, you will have forgotten your day-to-day issues, discomforts, and worries by concentrating on the well-being of others, which you will have accomplished without even recognizing it. And that is priceless.

SOMETIMES, LESS IS MUCH MORE

From a very young age, our brain is inundated with advertising of automobiles, beautiful people, colognes, more beautiful people, and various types of automobiles, among other things. They are a visual stimulation that, as we discussed in the chapter titled "High Vibration," are progressively deposited in our subconscious, changing the nature of our mind and making us hungry to consume, alter, purchase, throw away... and buy again. This is because of the way that our mind works. Don't get me wrong. It's always a good idea to be open to new experiences and opportunities, especially if you're not happy with who or where you are right now. But if you appear to have "everything," there will come a moment when you give in to routine and boredom, or become unmotivated, and you will stop recognizing and valuing all the wonderful things that are around you. Then, in an effort to recapture that sense of freshness and excitement, you might make the decision to give up all you've worked so hard to achieve over the past several years and start over from scratch. You forsake what you love and what you have had for such a significant amount of time in order to have for a brief moment what you "want," or more accurately, what you think you desire. And all of this is down to the never-ending barrage of stimulus that feeds into your already-existing feelings of dissatisfaction and agitates your already-present anxiety. That is the kind of change I was referring to, although I believe it is more accurately referred to as involution rather than change.

Also, in the chapter titled "*Pleasure for pleasure's sake*", we discussed how essential it is to avoid basing our "happiness" on fleeting and superficial pleasures. This is because we will always be reliant on an external source in order to feel that momentary "well-being" that pleasure provides.

Once more, I want to make it clear that indulging in pleasure is not inherently sinful as long as we do not let it control our lives and do not let it become an object of abuse or an obsession. Everyone will have a good handle on sexual activity, alcoholic beverages, and financial matters. However, if we make something that can provide us with momentary relief in some circumstances the sole source of relief in our lives, there will come a time when it will provide the opposite effect. One day, our so-called "well-being" will consist entirely of our bodies, and we'll feel depressed, empty, and unmotivated inside our heads.

I have personal experience with folks who were born into wealthy families but by the time they were 30 years old were suffering from depression, alcoholism, or other serious vices.

Let us ponder these words, for I believe they represent a very significant piece of advice:

"Happiness is not in obtaining what you want; rather, it is in wanting what you already have".

Confucius

A path that leads nowhere is paved with overstimulation, and more specifically, the fixation or desire to acquire more and more material stuff. Or, more precisely, it does not lead anywhere that is worthwhile. If we strive to acquire ever more things, we will eventually come to see nothing as valuable. And because we keep going around counting stars, we will end up losing the moon."

It is not about having the mindset that we have less things; rather, it is about having the mindset that we have everything.

Even if we continue to want something else or want to accomplish more goals, we must always be grateful so that we do not forget where we came from and the great abundance that surrounds us and of which we are a part on a daily basis. This will prevent us from forgetting where we came from and the great abundance that is available to us.

There will always be someone with less than us who is content with their lives, and there will always be someone with more than us who is miserable with their lives. Because of this, we need to be aware of how fortunate we are simply to be here and now, reading this book, in a private moment of calm and inner search, investigating, evolving, and gaining a greater understanding about this wonderful and complex mechanism in which it has been bestowed upon us to live, our being.

If we knew all the tricks, the fun would be gone; if everything was easy, it would be dull; if we had all the riches in the world, a different "love" every night, and all of the money, sex, and vices that you could possibly dream, nothing would be worth it. Nothing would be worth the time, work, and sacrifice that it requires, not to mention the amount of willpower that is required. How then could we place a value on it?

There is a proverb that states, "What comes easily, departs easily," which may also be interpreted to mean that whatever that was simple to obtain, whether it was simpler than expected or not, will eventually disappear. If we haven't had to put in any effort or sacrifice, if it hasn't been "hard" for us, if we haven't had to concentrate and pay attention, if we haven't had to give up our free time in order to get it done, then it won't mean anything. If we haven't put in any of those things, then it won't mean anything. A mental marker will be placed in our heads as if to say, "Ha, I got it quickly and easily, I can have it whenever I want, and there will be many more just like this one." Then you will believe that if it does not work for you, you can take another and another without pausing to appreciate the experience or value anything, and you will continue to believe this even if it does not work for you.

I came to the conclusion that a chapter with the heading "Less is more" would be beneficial for a number of reasons, including this one. In spite of the fact that it can appear to be a straightforward idea that can be summed up in a few sentences, many people find it challenging to assimilate.

"Less is more" does not mean believing that you have very little; rather, it means having the attitude that what you do have is sufficient; it means being grateful for what you are and what you have; it means being conscious of the abundance of love and beauty that is all around us.

That is why I use the word "think" when I write "think you have little," and that is why I use the word "feel" when I write "feel that what you have is enough," because thinking does not have to imply consciousness on your part; we all think every day without having to be part of that "action," and most of the time thinking happens without us having to do anything at all. That is why I use the word "feel" when I write "feel that what you have is enough."

But emotion is a completely different matter. Even if we don't perceive it that way, most of the time we are making a choice, even if we don't realize it. After that comes feeling, and after that is a sense. First I think, whether consciously or unconsciously. It takes more participation on our part.

If a thought occurs to us out of the blue and we give it our full attention for a predetermined amount of time, we make the conscious decision to feel a particular way, and this results in a sensation that can be either positive or negative, depending on the nature of the thought and the extent to which we can visualize it.

Exercise:

Look at everything that is going on in your life: do you have a home, a family, a job, friends, a partner, do you eat more than once a day, are you healthy, do you have free time, can you exercise, read, or go to a new restaurant? You then have access to significantly more than 75% of the whole population.

Take a deep breath in and gently say out loud "I appreciate this moment and the experience I am receiving" as you feel the power of the words of thankfulness you are reading. Thank you.

I am fortunate in that I have a home, food, my health, a job, friends, and love. As a result of my great good fortune and the fact that I am surrounded by plenty, I don't require anything else to be happy. Happiness has already found me. I lead a good life.

As I take a breath, a grin spreads across my face. In addition, I do everything I can to ensure the happiness of those around me.

Thank you very much, world. Thank you air. I appreciate the bright sunshine. I am grateful to life.

I pray with all of my heart that the power of these words resonates with you and permeates your being. Keep in mind that you can reinforce something in your mind by repeating these affirmations whenever you want, as well as others that you develop yourself, in order to strengthen something. The power lies not only in the words themselves, but also in the meaning they convey and the perspective from which they are read.

You have a lot of power. One of the many ways in which your mind possesses the capacity to bring inner calm and contentment to you is the one that you have just realized. Never forget the power that you possess.

We enjoy a privileged position. As I was saying earlier, sadness and boredom are issues that are more common in the first world, or the West. Only here are we so easily diverted by so many external stimuli that we are unable to pause for a few minutes and breathe slowly and deeply in order to get a sense of our bodies, to train our minds to slow down, and to nurture our own sense of serenity.

THE METHOD TO ACHIEVE ABUNDANCE

The concept of abundance may sound like having a lot of money, living a lavish lifestyle, and frittering it away. However, it is also a spiritual term that may be used to describe all of the positive things that come our way and are all around us. Having the realization that we are blessed leads to feelings of thankfulness, having those feelings of gratitude leads to feelings of pleasure, and having those feelings of happiness is the secret to having abundance.

Because there isn't as much going on in the wilderness as there is in the city, city dwellers may find that being in the center of nature is uninteresting. On the other hand, being in a mountain may be an absolutely mind-blowing adventure for someone else who comes from the same town, the same neighborhood, or even the same family as you. The same location of birth, very identical DNA—so what's different? Those parts of the body that take in the scenery, the angle of view, and the impression.

Whatever it is that we give our attention to grows in our lives. If we dwell on the negative, we are sending the world the message that we take pleasure in the negative, which will result in the manifestation of additional negative occurrences. On the other side, if we choose to think positively and appreciate all that makes us who we are and everything that is around us, we will experience a life filled with plenty.

If I take a stroll around the park, I may find myself dwelling on the stressful events of the previous day at work, how little I look forward to reporting for duty the following day, and the amount of time I have left to complete that challenging undertaking... And all of a sudden, something unpleasant happens to us; either we step in dog feces, or we get a scare when crossing the street because we were not paying attention and did not look at both sides of the road before we crossed, or the phone rings, and someone tells us some unfavorable information. It would appear that this was done on purpose. Since when does one horrible thing happen to you, and then it feels like just behind it follows another, and then another, and then another..... However, this is not the case; rather, it is due to the fact that our internal filter causes us to concentrate solely on the negative aspects of the situation while ignoring any and all positive aspects.

Possibly, if we hadn't been so preoccupied with our own thoughts as we strolled through the park, we would have noticed what a wonderful day it was, or those curious flowers that had grown on the side of the road, or that little girl who was playing with her dog and dying of laughter every time I brought the ball back to her. Those are all things that we might have noticed if we hadn't been so preoccupied with our own thoughts.

What you desire to see is what life is. It is a combination of unplanned occurrences that are precisely arranged together with your perspective and the way you look at things in the world.

They say that attitude is everything, and those people are not incorrect in the least. One person may find a particular occurrence tedious or unappealing, whereas another may find it fascinating and intensely pleasurable. Yes, we are all unique; nevertheless, if I am unable to recognize, value, and express gratitude for the tremendous wealth that is all around me, then shouldn't I make an effort to alter my way of thinking in order to be able to do so?

"They tell of a wise man who, at one point in his life, fell into disgrace and became so impoverished that the only thing that kept him alive were the herbs he harvested. Will there be anyone, he asked himself, who is less fortunate and more unfortunate than me?

And as soon as he turned his head, there it was in front of him: another wise man was picking the herbs he had been throwing away.

Complaining about my lot in life I lived in this world, and when I asked myself: Is there another person with worse fortune? I realized that the answer was no.

Because, upon coming back to my senses, I've realized that you would have gathered my woes in order to turn them into delights".

Pedro Calderón de la Barca "La vida es sueño" (Life is a dream) 17th century

What some people consider to be leftovers, others consider to be food. What might be an unpleasant experience for you could be an opportunity for growth for someone else. Some people's idea of hell is another person's idea of work and willpower. And if, after reading these lines, you still are unable to recognize the bounty that is all around us, as other people do, then you should be another. Change. Meditate, grow, educate yourself, and transform your being. Take another role. Be the person you envision yourself to be. The person who finds delight in a cloudy day just as much as in a sunny day, the person who can put a grin on the face of someone who is having a bad day and make their day better. the person who offers assistance without anticipating receiving anything in return. I am aware of who you would like to become; but, if you are not there yet, you should get started right away because there is very little time left to understand that what has been lost was the most important thing in your life. The moments, the adventures, the feelings, the hilarity, the companionship, and the life itself. Someone else will experience it in your place if you are not here to do so. However, it will not be you; rather, it will be another person. If you can't smile at a stranger, if you don't like this day, no matter how it looks, if you're sick of your job and you're still at it, if you can't laugh out loud for no reason, then be someone else.

There is much available in every shape and setting. It is sustenance; it is fuel; it is energy; it is love; it is melody; it is joy; it is life. It's when you meet someone for the first time and immediately feel like you've known them before thanks to their wonderful chat. It's like you're wandering down a strange street then all of a sudden you spot a restaurant serving cuisine from a different culture and decide to go in there so you can try out some unusual flavors. It's when you find a new artist and instantly fall in love with practically all of their tracks. When you visit a foreign nation for the first time and find that you have a positive impression of the culture and would enjoy living there, you have experienced abundance. But none of this will occur if you are unable to appreciate the abundance that is before you and if all you can see in the sky is gloomy clouds. There are times when things do not even exist, yet we make them up nevertheless. mostly due to the fact that we thought, act, and materialize. Therefore, we are, to some part, the creators of the reality that we experience. In school, we were never shown how to draw our lives or write our destinies, but it's never too late to pick up new skills; learning is something you can do at any point in your life.

Exercise:

When you get off work or when the day is over, go to your house and find somewhere comfy to sit. Take a few slow, deep breaths to calm yourself down. Please take a moment to open your go-to journal or notebook and jot down the current date. Put in writing two positive experiences you had today, whether they were words other people said to you or feelings you had, things that happened to you or things you noticed. Something fresh and uplifting to look forward to. If you feel confident, write more, as many as you want. Now read them again, what feeling do they give you?

Repeat this exercise every day for a month. In this way, we are educating your mind to focus on the good in our life. In this way we eliminate negativity and depression or dissatisfaction. By doing so, we cultivate an awareness of the limitless abundance that is all around us and of which we are a part in every moment of our lives.

AN OBJECTIVE READING OF THE SITUATION

It is inevitable, or rather, it is almost impossible, for us to pass judgment on something when we see the actions of another person or are told a story about something that has just taken place. We may judge it to be good, right, wrong, or horrible, but it almost never manages to apathetically pass us by. It is necessary for us to voice our opinion. It is how we expose our ideals and defend who we are, how we empathize with others or differentiate ourselves, and how we express ourselves. And you are not wrong in the least. When we create something good, that is, when we establish in our mind that a fact or a concept is correct, or that to achieve something determined is ideal, when we do this without wanting it, we are also creating something bad, because we give life to its opposite. This is a very interesting thing to think about. To put it another way, the fact that we have not yet accomplished the positive goal that we have set for ourselves is a drawback. For instance, if we had the intention of completing our degree (something positive) but were unable to do so (something negative) due to unforeseen circumstances, such as our father falling ill and requiring us to begin working before we could do so, we would have negative emotions. Because the thing that was supposed to make us feel good did not come true or we did not obtain it, we are not in a good mood. Unconsciously, we have trained our minds with the concept that it is unethical for us to obtain the opposite of what we desired or to not get the excellent thing that we wanted. This has led us to believe that it is bad for us to have any of these outcomes. It's pretty uncommon to hear people say things like, "I didn't obtain that job that I wanted," "I'm thirty years old and I'm not married yet," "I wanted to have had children before I was thirty-five," and other similar statements.

Obviously, these are aggravating truths that anyone would find annoying or choose to ignore for the time being. There are also deeds that are without a doubt wicked and there is no other way to look at them, such as crimes, homicides, sexual assaults, and a long list of further examples. That is something that cannot be contested. But the realities of our day-to-day existence are what really matter to us in this context.

Because we must confront the human mental conditioning that has taken its toll on us for centuries, it will be necessary to be very aware of our unconscious reactions in order to successfully apply the concept of neutral interpretation, despite the fact that its explanation is straightforward and its application is challenging.

A neutral interpretation involves keeping one's personality and one's sense of judgment in check so that one may recognize that something is neither positive nor negative; rather, it simply IS. Believe me when I say that this is already a positive development. It entails distancing oneself from the mind and the deceptions it can produce, as well as preventing the mind from forming judgements that take us in the wrong direction or do us no benefit.

For instance, if I were driving on the road and someone were to cross the road in front of me in a hazardous manner, I would sound the horn to give him an audible warning. If he then suddenly changes lanes and brakes, reaches my height and shouts at me, insults me, or makes aggressive hand gestures, I could follow his energetic current and shout at him and insult him too, making me an accomplice of his bad behavior and paying, at least energetically, the consequences of his mistakes. Because I am not able to give the road my complete attention while I am angry, I am increasing the likelihood that I will be the one to cause an accident. This could wind up being an even worse problem.

However, we may also just take a few deep breaths, smile, and make a gesture that expresses our regret for whatever happened, even if it wasn't even our fault, and then continue on our way without any further issues. This manner, we would prevent their negative energy from affecting and contaminating us, and we would be able to continue on our journey without being damaged while maintaining the purity of our vibration. If you do not let something affect you, then it cannot. According to a well-known proverb, "*it is not he who wants to offend but he who can*". However, you should not give them the opportunity to upset you. It is not about taking a defensive stance; it is about fighting back. It is a matter of acceptance and letting go of attachments. Recognize that conduct as being pointless and then send it back to where it came from.

"While the master monk and his student were strolling down the street, an assailant suddenly appeared from behind and viciously attacked the monk, causing him to fall to the ground.

Master! -the terrified student yelled out to his master as he pulled his master to his feet and asked: "are you okay?"

The elderly monk quietly got to his feet, dusted down his robe, and continued on his way without making any kind of a fuss, emotion, or complaint of any kind.

The student cried out loud to the teacher: but master! Who was that man? You didn't even bother to look in his direction, and you have no idea who he is or why he did what he did!

It's not my problem; it's his -said the professor calmly.

A story from the oral history of the Zen tradition

The problem is not ours until such time as we choose to take responsibility for it by responding in a negative manner. It is not required to react; rather, it is necessary to act, which involves accepting what occurs and allowing it to pass or ignoring it. However, there are situations in which it is not even necessary to act.

In no way, shape, or form does any of this have anything to do with humbling oneself or permitting oneself to be mistreated by another person. In real life, there is almost never an absolute right or wrong answer; instead, there are a variety of shades of gray.

"Would you keep the remaining 86340 euros in your possession if someone stole 60 of them from you? Wouldn't you say no to that? Now suppose that instead of having 86400 euros, you have 86400 seconds, which is the same number of seconds that make up one day. So, tell me, would you squander the 86340 seconds that you have left after someone wastes 60 seconds of your time with their negative attitude or their terrible intentions?"

Text taken from Marc Levy's book "Et si c'était vrai (And if it were true)," which was published

in the year 2000, and subsequently translated and edited by Levy.

Take into consideration the following: When you are next overcome with hate or resentment because of someone's impolite behavior or abuse, take a moment to ponder on whether it is worth wasting an entire day on being angry or resentful just because someone wasted a minute of your time with impolite words, intents, or manners.

Exercise:

Simply remove yourself from the situation if you are being tormented by negative energies, are subjected to severe criticism, or feel that your emotional or energetic balance is in jeopardy. Do not interpret it, do not accuse, and do not judge it in any manner, regardless of whether it is feasible to walk away or not. Focus your attention on your breath and become aware of your body. You have the ability to tell yourself things like, "You are not mine, you do not belong to me, and I do not want you here."

Or, you may just say, "It won't get me anything in the end!"

Or, you may say something like, "We appreciate your participation! You should expect to hear from us in the near future.

You are the one who brings into existence everything that you desire or do not desire to have in your life, and you are also the one who brings it all to an end. Make the most of your ideas and don't give them the opportunity to take advantage of you; believe me when I say that they will if they find no one steering the ship when they arrive. Use your thoughts to your advantage.

LAW OF ATTRACTION

I will never get tired of saying that we are creative beings because it is the truth. As was mentioned in the previous chapter titled "High Vibration," our ideas serve as the raw material from which our dreams are constructed. We have the ability to take something that is formless and ethereal and transform it into something that is concrete and material that exists in the real world. If we make the decision to study a career because we want to be, for example, a journalist, we will have to attend school for a number of years, study, take examinations, and then ultimately earn the degree. We are going to look for jobs, and ultimately, we are going to find ourselves working as journalists. We've made it. Something that had previously just been a concept in our heads became a fact as a result of our actions.

The vast majority of us are completely oblivious to the magnitude of this power. We were not shown it or instructed on how to use it when we were children. Nevertheless, throughout the course of our lives, there are times when we come to the realization that there is something more shaping our lives than the outcomes of random or chance occurrences. You were reflecting on an old acquaintance who you hadn't spoken to in a few weeks when all of a sudden, he gives you a call. Or you meet someone for the first time, and then the next day you run into them again somewhere else, or you're looking for a job and someone offers you a one-of-a-kind chance while you're having a conversation with them, and so on. Synchronicity is the term that Carl Jung used to describe what some people refer to as chance or causality.

The word "yes" is communicated by the universe through the phenomenon of synchronicity. It's how you know you're spending your time with the right person at the right place at the right moment. If you make the most of that opportunity, you will undoubtedly learn something important or be in a position to instruct or assist another person in some way. When you find yourself wondering "how is that possible, what a coincidence!," then it is the perfect time to be completely attentive and sensitive to what is occurring around you. It's possible that something extraordinary may take place, like an opportunity to advance professionally or emotionally, or even both.

Our subconscious regulates our existence. During our time here on Earth, we are exposed to a plethora of stimuli, experiences, and memories, all of which contribute to the programming of our unconscious selves. All of this knowledge contributes to the construction of a singular aspect of our identity, a personal perspective that determines how we respond, if at all, to the happenings of daily life. This unconsciously occurring chain of impulses or instinctive reactions has a decisive impact on our viewpoint of the world and modifies the manner in which we perceive the things that are in our immediate environment.

If we had a difficult childhood, we may mistrust someone who wants to open up to us or who treats us well. On the other hand, we may, at the slightest opportunity we see to trust someone, do it blindly and without waiting for that trust to be generated naturally, which may cause the other person to become scared and run away.

Because this has always been the case, a significant portion of our lives are fully controlled by the unconscious, but we are not aware of this fact. What if, on the other hand, we were able to build a happier and more optimistic version of ourselves by naturally influencing our subconscious? That is not impossible, but it will take hard work and dedication on your part, just like practically everything worthwhile in life.

"The ideal society is just around the corner. When I take two steps, the object moves two steps further away, and 10 more steps are covered by the horizon. So, what exactly is the point of utopia? Walking is the primary purpose of this".

Eduardo Galeano

It is not going to happen in the wink of an eye or overnight that we will become the best versions of ourselves. If we did that, it wouldn't accomplish much, and after a while we'd probably start feeling bored of it, at which point we'd revert to the way things were before. It takes years for wine to age properly. Time, affection, mutual comprehension, and attention to detail are the building blocks of a healthy relationship. It takes more than just water to make a tree robust and lush; it also takes time and love. Let us therefore not have the expectation that we will be able to fix all of our behavioral or perceptual issues in a flash.

When I have a bad thinking, or when anything encourages me to focus on things that are unfair or that do nothing for me, I like to remember a statement that I have read some time ago and that goes like this:

"It is not possible to achieve perfection in everything. If you can learn to accept it, then everything will work out perfectly".

Chris Diaz

What ought to be flawless is not the physical environment in which we live, but rather our methods of seeing and valuing it. We all make mistakes, and sometimes in nature things happen that, depending on our point of view, can appear to be extremely cruel and destructive. But the way you look at the world determines how you see it, not the other way around.

If you alter the way in which you perceive the world, the world around you will also shift.

Exercise: If we want to achieve a large or long-term goal, it is highly useful and crucial to create those smaller tasks or goals necessary to reach the end objective. Setting these smaller goals and tasks is the key to success. Together, we will make significant progress over time. To go someplace, walking is the most efficient mode of transportation. Learning and growing as an individual is a journey that is sure to be enjoyable. A small percentage of people have the guts to go on this journey to evolve in many facets of their lives.

In the first blank page of your brand-new, glistening, and potent notebook, jot down the title of a significant goal that you have set for yourself. Your ideal work, your life plan, your athletic objectives, your perfect home, your independence from monetary worries... now write down, beneath that significant title, all of the smaller goals or tasks that are required to attain your ultimate objective. Don't be sloppy with the specifics. You should now be aware that the goal you have set for yourself has a significant value, and that you will be thankful for it once you have accomplished it. As you complete the smaller tasks listed in the notebook on a day-to-day basis, you will move closer to achieving your overall objective. Study, do research, talk to people who already know about or are succeeding in something similar, and version what they did to succeed in order to figure out what they did to get there. If there is somewhere you feel that you are not making progress, try new strategies and different ways to achieve it. Simply committing it to paper is the first step in turning it into a concrete plan that can eventually become a reality.

Daily, out loud, repeat what it is you want to do and the reasons behind your desire for it, and act as if you have already accomplished it. Visualize yourself in that circumstance, having successfully completed your goal, and do so in great detail. Imagine what you would wear, how you would talk, the house you would live in, and most importantly, how you would feel if all of these things were true. You should write everything down and then read it aloud as though you already knrw everything. Without hesitating, with enthusiasm and determination. If you combine all of these strategies, you will be able to accomplish everything you set your mind to. Feel the power of creativity flowing outward from within you as you practice gratitude for this entire process of development. Becoming a magnet for whatever it is that you want to bring into your life can be accomplished by following the steps outlined above.

If you have the willpower and the determination, you can accomplish everything you set your mind to.

TRY TO FEEL MORE AND THINK LESS

Observe how the passage of time seems to fly by, how you come up with the finest jokes, how appreciative and joyful you are, and how you share that positive energy and affection with everyone else around you once you get some good news and celebrate it. There is no room in this busy schedule for your mind to intrude with its never-ending babbling and incessant babbling of empty thoughts. We are so preoccupied with living in the here and now, in the now, or, what amounts to the same thing, thinking less and feeling more, that we have little time to dwell on the past or the future. And don't you think it would be incredible to spend the entirety of your life, or at least the most of it, in a state of bliss similar to this?

That is certainly a possibility if we focus our attention and pay attention to the times in our lives when we are operating on "autopilot" and the times when we have complete control over what we are doing. If we allow ourselves to become sidetracked by things like thinking about our concerns or issues, gazing at our mobile phones or the television, our minds work for us, and we have very little control over how they operate. Our respect for reality wanes, and we fall into a cycle of apathy, indifference, and, most importantly, a diminished capacity for original thought and productive endeavor.

If, on the other hand, we are completely absorbed in an activity, a sport, an exciting work, or a meaningful conversation with another person, then we are living in the here and now; we are more SOUL than MIND; we are thinking less and feeling more. It is a form of meditation in action because we are preventing the mind from polluting the moment with its regular interferences and we are letting our passion and creativity run wild. This is how I choose to look at things, and it is the perspective that has been the most helpful to me in directing my attention and efforts toward living in the here and now, which is where everything takes place.

You can heal your soul by devoting a portion of your energy to the cultivation of your mind. When we become aware of the fact that thoughts arise spontaneously in our heads, without a reason or trigger, and that many times these thoughts do not bring us anything or lead us to act or react in a negative way, we have taken the first step toward becoming aware. We are feeling. Our hearts are leading our minds at this point. When we have that aha! moment and realize that our unconscious mind does not represent who we are, but our conscious mind does, we have entered the magical realm. Since it is because of it that we have choice, being conscious is how we arrive at the best options, when we mix reason and experience, thoughts and feelings, mind and soul. Because it is because of it that we have choice. If everything were driven by instinct rather than consciousness, then we would still be animals and be forced to murder ourselves in order to stay alive.

Possibly, there are times when we are unable to choose what to think about because the dish has already been set before us. However, we can choose what to "feed," which means that we can choose which thoughts to pay attention to, which ones are worth developing, and which ones require us to devote time to them that we will never get back.

Let's look at it from this perspective: Something that isn't good for me, something that might not have even happened, a dread or a worry that I have is running through my head right now. When we picture something, the tremendous power of our minds makes it seem as though it is really taking place. Our bodies put every cell to work on that concept, and the entire emotion, whether it is positive or bad, floods and controls us. The body becomes flooded with hormones that are created as a result of the emotions, and as a result, we lose awareness of what we are thinking and enter a feedback loop. Don't let that happen. You are free to terminate the process whenever you like. Because once an emotion has reached our heads, logical reasoning vanishes, the majority of the time, we are emotional animals as opposed to intellectual animals.

Consider some of the unfavorable feelings that have been responsible for so much devastation on the planet: Envy, religious fanaticism, power, abuse, and control, greed—all of these things go nowhere good and consume the person who has them to the core. Greed, an endless hunger for money and corruption, religious fanaticism; power, abuse, and control

Exercise: When we have a thought that does not make us happy and someone comes on our door, let us not worry, let us not feel, let us not give it worth or meaning, and let us not pay more attention to it than is absolutely necessary. As it came, let it pass. You ought to concentrate on anything else instead. To this point, we have discussed a variety of strategies throughout this book to help you focus your mind on the here and now, and I believe you currently possess the tools necessary to get started on accomplishing this goal. It may all be summed up as follows: when a bad unconscious idea enters your mind, immediately replace it with a positive conscious thought. If you are having negative thoughts, counteract them by taking positive action. To put it another way, don't go along for the journey that your mind is taking you on; instead, steer it in the direction that you want it to go. Use the techniques described in the previous chapters, such as touching the wall and feeling how it feels, touching your body and seeing how it feels, touching your clothes and seeing how they feel, focusing on your breathing, singing, humming, talking out loud, saying "I don't care, thank you and good day," exercising, and writing in your power notebook "nothing bad stays with me." And then, just as quickly as you can process the information, it will be gone. You can accomplish this goal in a few different ways; select the approach that strikes a chord with you, the one that seems most natural to you, or the one that most makes sense to you.

These strategies for living in the here and now are by no means exhaustive, nor are they the only ones that can be employed. There are probably a lot more, and as you go along, you might even find some new ones or come up with some new ones. The approaches outlined in this article are the ones that were successful for me and continue to be beneficial to me to this day. I sincerely want that they relieve some of your burden and make it possible for you to soar with greater ease.

I am grateful that you are present right now.

FINAL REFLECTION

Your inner trip of self-improvement and development may have just begun, or may have already proceeded all the way to the end of the road, but the voyage through this book has come to a successful conclusion.

One of the many things that makes life so beautiful is the ability to draw sustenance from one's surroundings in order to grow and develop on multiple fronts. When we feel that anything is bothering us, having the ability to go inward can offer us a greater understanding of how our feelings, our health, our mind, and our soul work.

If we feed our minds with nutritious and uplifting thoughts, we will find that doing so has many great effects on our lives. Our levels of energy and willpower, as well as our focus and mood, will both see significant improvements. We will also have better sleep, and as a result, we will have a wonderful day, which will lead to the creation of a cycle of well-being that will considerably improve the quality of our lives.

In a similar vein, if we make an effort to be selective about the thoughts to which we give our attention and ensure that only those that contribute something beneficial to our lives continue to flourish, then our state of mind will be more at ease and free of worry and anxiety. We will be able to perform more effectively at work, our capacity to make judgments will increase, we will have a more optimistic outlook, and a host of other benefits.

"An elderly Native American was having a conversation with his grandson by the warmth of the campfire. He said that within everyone of us, there is a battle between two wolves. There is one of them that is a furious, vicious, and vindictive wolf. The other person is overflowing with love, gratitude, and compassion for others.

The grandchild inquired: which of the two of you do you think would prevail in the fight, Grandfather?

In response, Grandfather said: the one I take care of".

Ancient Cherokee tale

We should not blame ourselves for what we think unconsciously; rather, we should accept responsibility for what we feel, as this takes more participation on our part than what we think unconsciously. A thought may appear spontaneously, but by giving it our undivided attention, we give it the opportunity to grow in power and sophistication. Make an informed decision about the aspects of yourself that you want to develop.

In a similar fashion, our soul cries out for the necessary amount of "nutrition." The soul will feel at ease, happy, and grateful if we take care of our mind in a variety of ways, and we will be able to turn to it at times when our mind "betrays" us. When we are able to fully immerse ourselves in the present now without allowing ourselves to be sidetracked by anything else, we are able to access our soul, which is the place within us where everything is perfect, where there are no disruptions or issues, stress or pain.

Feeling comes from the soul, whereas thinking comes from the mind. If we make the decision to solely entertain and cultivate happy thoughts, then the soul will provide us with sensations and sentiments of happiness and overall well-being. It might not be as easy as it seems to put into practice, just like everything else worthwhile in life that can be appreciated over the course of a lifetime. Once you have an understanding of your true power, every stage of your life will present you with opportunities to grow and enjoy abundance. You shouldn't pass up the chance to improve the quality of your life.

Whenever you feel stressed or anxious, or when you find yourself thinking too much, bring your attention back to your body and remember to take slow, deep breaths. The same energy that makes you angry is also the energy that might help you relax and feel better. You merely need to acquire the skills necessary to control it and work it to your benefit.

I am grateful that you decided to read my book

I truly wish that you have found the voyage through the pages of this book to be enjoyable, and that the lessons and motivation that you have gained from reading about my experiences will assist you in your own road toward personal development, mental health, and happiness.

Help me to help

The most helpful thing you could do for me would be to provide a review or rating of my book on the website where you purchased it, preferably one that is good. It won't take you more than a few seconds to do, but completing it would mean a great deal to me.

If you give my work a positive rating, it will be able to reach more people and have a positive effect on their life, their health, and their well-being.

I hope that your travels are filled with joy, and that you find serenity and abundance.

Max Cureton

www.ingramcontent.com/pod-product-compliance
Lightning Source LLC
Chambersburg PA
CBHW050251010526
44107CB00003B/272